HUNTING

The MIT Press Essential Knowledge Series

A complete list of books in this series can be found online at
https://mitpress.mit.edu/books/series/mit-press-essential-knowledge-series.

HUNTING

A CULTURAL HISTORY

JAN E. DIZARD AND
MARY ZEISS STANGE

The MIT Press | Cambridge, Massachusetts | London, England

The MIT Press would like to thank the anonymous peer reviewers who provided comments on drafts of this book. The generous work of academic experts is essential for establishing the authority and quality of our publications. We acknowledge with gratitude the contributions of these otherwise uncredited readers.

This book was set in Chaparral Pro by New Best-set Typesetters Ltd. Printed and bound in the United States of America.

Library of Congress Cataloging-in-Publication Data

Names: Dizard, Jan E., 1940- author. | Stange, Mary Zeiss, author.
Title: Hunting : a cultural history / Jan E. Dizard and Mary Zeiss Stange.
Description: Cambridge, Massachusetts : The MIT Press, [2022] | Series: The MIT Press Essential Knowledge Series | Includes bibliographical references and index.
Identifiers: LCCN 2021051213 | ISBN 9780262543293 (Paperback)
Subjects: LCSH: Hunting.
Classification: LCC GT5810 .D59 2022 | DDC 306.4/83—dc23/eng/20211022
LC record available at https://lccn.loc.gov/2021051213

10   9   8   7   6   5   4   3   2   1

CONTENTS

SERIES FOREWORD

The MIT Press Essential Knowledge series offers accessible, concise, beautifully produced pocket-size books on topics of current interest. Written by leading thinkers, the books in this series deliver expert overviews of subjects that range from the cultural and the historical to the scientific and the technical.

In today's era of instant information gratification, we have ready access to opinions, rationalizations, and superficial descriptions. Much harder to come by is the foundational knowledge that informs a principled understanding of the world. Essential Knowledge books fill that need. Synthesizing specialized subject matter for nonspecialists and engaging critical topics through fundamentals, each of these compact volumes offers readers a point of access to complex ideas.

FOREWORD

MAN, THE HUNTER?

We begin this story of hunting with an image. It's a picture worth at least a thousand words. We have all likely seen some version of it, and we know (or at least we think we do) the story behind it. A series of figures process across the otherwise vacant page. First in line, and by implication first in time, is a knuckle-walking apelike creature, suggesting something between a chimp and baboon. Next comes a hairy, slope-shouldered prehominid, empty-handed and likely empty-headed, but managing to get along on two feet and apparently aware of his surroundings. The next figure, his successor, has evolved sufficiently to have a name, *Homo erectus*, and he looks to be a missing link of sorts; fully erect, but still apelike, he is naked, and his hands are empty. There may or may not be a few extras thrown into the parade at this point, but the visual emphasis now shifts to the final two figures, both of them human. One is an erect, fur-clad Neanderthal, clutching a club or stone axe, yet with a look of bewilderment that clearly indicates he is too dim-witted to survive for long in this complicated world he has inherited. But then finally, one might well say triumphantly, our primitive human is overtaken by a more recognizably human model. This is the man whose physique is well muscled, and his attention is focused sharply ahead. Brandishing a flint-tipped spear, he radiates leadership potential. This man strides confidently off the page and into the future. This is *Homo sapiens sapiens*. And he, in a word, is us.

Or so the story once went, buttressed by invoking naturalist Charles Darwin's evolutionary theory, though it's unlikely Darwin would have endorsed so linear a model. These little pictographs, which still grace a fair share of high school biology texts, generally bear a title such as "The Ascent of Man" or "The Evolution of Man." And by the mid-twentieth century, the version of human evolution they represented was held to be powerfully supported by developments in the field of anthropology—cultural advances to which hunting seemed to contribute. We humans had been hunting for as long as we had been humans—that much was clear and reasonably well supported by the anthropological evidence.

But did hunting make us human? In the post–World War II, Cold War heyday of what came to be called the "hunting hypothesis of human origins," the answer seemed

Did hunting make us human?

obviously "yes." The line of reasoning was elegant in its simplicity. In our earlier evolutional history, our protoprimate predecessors spent the bulk of their time hanging out in trees, swinging from limb to limb, and snacking on fruits, nuts, and berries. Those ancestors eventually descended from the trees and learned to forage for a widening menu of culinary choices. Along the way, they became "killer apes" and developed bipedalism, which allowed them to venture ever farther out and about in their green world.[1] With upright posture came far better visual acuity, and along with that the ability to think and act in spatial terms, plan and act cooperatively, communicate both verbally and via sign language, and invent as well as create tools and weapons of various kinds. All of these behaviors that characterized early human social and cultural activity, it was held, derived from hunting. Moreover, the hunting hypothesis also explained the physiological and putative emotional differences between men and women.

Subsequent research and countertheorizing, however, rendered highly porous the argument that it was the complex of behaviors associated with hunting—more specifically, male hunting—that set the course of human evolution in the direction of *Homo sapiens sapiens* roughly two hundred thousand years ago. Anthropologists Richard Lee and Irven DeVore, whose massively influential anthology, aptly titled *Man the Hunter*, became something of a guidebook to the hunting hypothesis, acknowledged that their female colleagues raised some valid questions regarding the relative invisibility of women in the theory undergirding the hunting hypothesis.

Yet for them—and their colleagues who popularized the theory—in cross-cultural terms, hunting was so obviously and overwhelmingly "a male activity" that there was little real point in spending time, let alone research dollars, on questions relating to what the women might have been doing with their time and energy while the men were out bonding in the brush. Lee and DeVore granted that in evolutionary terms, it was "likely that early woman would not have remained idle during the Pleistocene" (a period of roughly 2.5 million years!), but nonetheless they saw little point in exploring whatever women may have been up to, while the male hunting bands were creating ever more efficient weaponry and beating the bush for meat.[2]

This much was clear, though: we could know, for a certainty, that for most of its time on earth up until about ten thousand years ago, humanity lived as hunter-foragers. We also know that the two oldest continuous human cultures on the planet—the Australian Aborigines and the peoples of the southern African desert, variously known as Khoi-San, Damara, and Bushmen—are historically hunter-foragers and still have ritual practices that relive that identity. And we know that while we may not be able to decipher all of its symbolism, the first great art our species produced, the cave art of the Upper Paleolithic,

represents a recognizably—indeed, startlingly familiar—
artistic sensibility. As the late paleontologist Stephen Jay
Gould remarked about sites like Lascaux in France and
Altamira in Spain, we are far closer in time to these Pleistocene painters than they were to those first *Homo sapiens
sapiens* who evolved on the African savanna two hundred
millennia ago. "These paintings speak so powerfully to us
because we know the people who did them," Gould declared. "They are us."[3]

Those people were hunters. As geographer Jared Diamond has pointed out, the images are drawn with a metic-
ulous knowledge of animal behavior and anatomy; some of
the bison at Lascaux are so finely detailed as to have tear
ducts.[4] The reason for this prehistoric naturalism is simple,
as any serious modern-day hunter could tell you. One cannot successfully hunt an animal one does not know and
know intimately. And as we show in the next chapter, the
hunt becomes embedded in increasingly rich layers of ritual that helped our ancestors to understand their relationship to the environments in which they found themselves.
Rituals played a crucial element in the hunting experience,
not least to mark in some ceremonial fashion the taking
of life toward the end of our own animal sustenance and
survival.

Whatever role it may or may not have played in humanity's biology, hunting indisputably both spurred and
shaped our cultural evolution. It inspired image and in-

Figure 1

vocation, song and story, ritual and dance, as humanity discerned its place in the larger scheme of things both mortal and immortal. And over time, our sense of place shifted from seeing ourselves as one with nature to seeing ourselves as *in* but not *of* nature; culture ("civilization") trumped nature (the "wild"). Artist Pablo Picasso is said to have been afforded an opportunity to visit the cave at Altamira that houses the first-discovered Pleistocene paintings of a bison herd galloping across the vaulted ceiling. Beholding here the work of kindred spirits, Picasso is reported to have exclaimed, "We have invented nothing new! After Altamira, all is decadence."[5] Still, there were many for whom these artworks represented at most child-like sketchings produced by childlike nomadic hunters, who—being hunters—were undoubtedly male. But one needed only to look at the ritual body painting and rock art practiced in some of the remotest places on earth by naked Aborigines and Koi-San trackers to see the similarities between then and now. That these contemporary hunters were overwhelmingly male—to the extent that women were forbidden to touch or even look at their artwork, let alone produce tools and hunting art of their own—well, that all simply made interpretative sense.

Feminist researchers were thus up against a formidable body of evidence and insight, marshaled by the male anthropological establishment. Anthropologist Hitoshi Watanabe summed up the essential evolutionary fact of gender difference simply: "Plants stand still, but animals move."[6] Women, being the supposedly weaker sex and more suitably adapted to a sedentary lifestyle, were clearly cut out for the tasks associated with gathering and little more. Reasoning along similar lines, in his widely influential book *The Naked Ape*, zoologist and painter Desmond Morris pointed out that all anybody needed to know about the "ascent of man" was,

> first, he had to hunt if he was to survive. Second,
> he had to have a better brain to make up for his

poor hunting body. Third, he had to have a longer childhood to grow the bigger brain and educate it. Fourth, the females had to stay put and mind the babies while the males went hunting. Fifth, the males had to cooperate with one another on the hunt. Sixth, they had to stand up straight and use weapons for the hunt to succeed.[7]

So then, as archaeologist Margaret Ehrenberg ventured to ask with thinly veiled sarcasm, was that *all* the ancient woman was doing? "Was she sitting at home, twiddling her thumbs, waiting for 'man' to feed her and increase his brain capacity and abilities until he became '*Homo sapiens sapiens?*'"[8] Or was she simply—and unwittingly—putting her evolutionary energies in the direction of evolving a broader pelvis to accommodate the larger brains of her more fully evolved male offspring? Although the lines between hunting and gathering are highly fungible, they scarcely seemed clear enough to hold the weight of the male-defined hunting hypothesis.

As the whose-hypothesis-is-better debate evolved, however, feminist researchers preferred to follow the logic—if not, strictly speaking, the lead—of their male colleagues. Observing that many of the same behaviors that drove the hunting hypothesis "worked" in the context of women's work too, they fashioned a counterhypothesis of human origins, focused on gathering. It therefore became possible to imagine hunting as a legitimate cross-gender activity in the same way that gathering was known to be. Over many millennia, it was clear that women—whose social role it was to maintain the seasonal encampment, tend to the children, and keep the home fires burning—also bore primary responsibility for foraging for a variety of foods that were relatively easy to capture via traps and snares, or harvest with primitive tools like digging sticks. This was work for which women appeared to be ideally suited. Along the way, they developed the science of horticulture.

There was, though, one aspect of hunting—and the lifeways of what would develop into hunting cultures—that depended on a signal difference between men and women—a difference on which the scholarly women and men of the mid- to late twentieth century agreed. It had to do with the apparently human—in fact, all *too* human—fact that people, especially male people, harbor a capacity for lethal violence. Indeed, when queried as to the role that killing plays in the "successful" hunt, the most ready-to-hand answer was the one supplied in another influential essay, "The Evolution of Hunting" by anthropologists Sherwood Washburn and C. S. Lancaster. In the coauthors' view, male violence came naturally. "Men enjoy hunting and killing," they argued, maintaining that

> part of the motivation for hunting is the immediate pleasure it gives the hunter. . . . Perhaps this is most

easily shown by the extent of the efforts devoted to maintain killing as a sport. . . . And until recently war was viewed in much the same way as hunting. . . . War has been far too important in human history for it to be other than pleasurable for the males involved.[9]

Given the overall thrust of this assertion, it is hardly surprising that feminist scholars—especially the more radically inclined among them—were finally happy to have something on which they could agree with their male colleagues. This was the "fact," ostensibly well established in radical and so-called cultural feminism, that males do indeed appear to enjoy hunting and killing. In effect, these feminist researchers were glad to let the men have that particular linchpin of their hunting hypothesis. Radical feminists Andree Collard and Joyce Contrucci put the case succinctly in *Rape of the Wild: Man's Violence against Animals and the Earth*. In their analysis, hunting led over time to the rise of "hunter kings," who luxuriated in the violence of wars, destroying nature, enslaving vanquished enemies, killing animals, raping women, and engaging in all forms of abuse and abasement. Women, meanwhile, enjoyed a range of "physical and spiritual connections" with nonhuman nature.[10] It was the more ethereally, soulfully inclined woman the gatherer who was the true originator of humanity.

Of course, the primal cavemen being long gone, it is important to realize whom, exactly, these scholar/researchers on both sides of the ideological fence were studying, and how. They were hunters—or more accurately, hunter-foragers. In his *The Empire of Nature: Hunting, Conservation, and British Imperialism*, historian John Mackenzie opts for a broad definition of these hunters' primary activity: "the pursuit, driving, ambushing, and trapping of wild animals of all species, with the intention of killing them for meat, other animal products, or purely for sport."[11]

But while this definition might capture a sense of the historical breadth and depth of hunting culture(s)—a subject to which we will return in subsequent chapters—it remains a fact that as Lee and DeVore acknowledged by the time anthropologists got around to studying them, "nowhere today do we find hunters living in a world of hunters." Indeed, as the "man the hunter" literature developed, there came to be general agreement, again quoting Lee and DeVore, that "the term 'hunters' is a convenient shorthand, despite the fact that the majority of peoples they considered subsisted primarily on sources *other than meat*—mainly wild plants and fish." Nonetheless hunting remained in their view the "master behavior pattern of the human species."[12]

As to the question of what the women were doing while the men were hunting, feminist researchers drew on various ways of characterizing the sexual division of labor to support their "gathering hypothesis" of human development. All of those facets of the male "master pattern," these researchers argued, would have been equally observable in female behaviors. And for reasons of efficiency, these women would have deferred to men when it suited their own nutritional and other ends. And that was that—or was it? In November 2020, it was reported that an archaeological site in Peru revealed a nine-thousand-year-old skeleton of a young female who was buried with the spear points and stone implements designed for skinning and flaying large animals. The researchers contended that "additional research shows something close to equal participation in hunting for both sexes. In general, they conclude 'early females in the Americas were big game hunters.'"[13]

As to evidence for the conventional view that men hunted and women gathered, researchers on both sides of the hunting versus gathering divide had two primary sources. One was the growing body of fossil evidence of the existence and lifeways of prehuman beings, like the skeletal remains of "Lucy," a 3.5-million-year-old Australopithecine lass, who was unearthed in Ethiopia in 1974 and became something of a paleontological superhero. The other was an intense anthropological focus on the few remaining hunter-forager cultures worldwide—primarily in the Australian outback and sub-Saharan Africa—the logic being that these contemporary hunter-gatherers are most likely to live and believe in ways suggesting a tradition thousands of years old. Both sources of information tended to support the conclusion that the grand trajectory of human history began with distant early ape-men and ape-women, and reached its epitome with—no surprise here—us.

It is certainly fair to argue that such research was based less on reading the fossil and human evidence than on reading *into* it—the logic being that one can look at fossil evidence using modern hunter-gatherer cultures as convenient points of comparison and see—to borrow the late anthropologist Michelle Rosaldo's wonderful phrasing—"the image of ourselves undressed."[14] Never mind that such surviving cultures as the Tiwi Aborigines of Australia, Philippine Agta, and Pygmies of the Congo are living cultures with beliefs and ritual practices of their own based on centuries-old cosmologies that are themselves very much alive. And as Lucy's discoverer, paleoanthropologist Donald Johanson, cautioned, "Only when we strip early humans of their future can we begin to understand the secrets of our past."[15]

Now, as we will presently see, those "secrets"—even and perhaps especially the ones that seem to be hiding in plain sight—are themselves constructions based on centuries and millennia of belief and practices that shore up our sense of how to go about living in a world that virtually any modern hunter-gatherer would tell you is still spirit filled—indeed, very much so.

Women largely disappeared from accounts of hunting, except in myths, until the era of British colonialism in India, Africa, and the Americas. While still overwhelmingly male, redoubtable women started to appear in accounts of life in the frontiers of the British colonies.

These exceptional women, though largely understudied still, nonetheless can be said to have helped pave the way for a relatively recent, significant growth in women's interest and participation in hunting. Interestingly, women from the nineteenth century to the present have also been leaders in the opposition to hunting, largely focusing their critique on how *men* who hunt are in various ways morally flawed, if not sadistic in pursuit of the kill. We will see in the chapters that follow how gender surfaces in the unfolding history of hunting.

Hunting has also been shaped by another characteristic that can be traced to our evolutionary origins, shared by many, if not most, species: a "pecking order." By all accounts, our foraging ancestors appear to have been remarkably egalitarian. To be sure, women were generally subordinate to men, though that should not be understood as women being passive. There are ample anthropological accounts of women who were anything but passive when men got out of line or the group's social order was threatened. And again generally, elders were accorded more say in the affairs of the group than were the young. But there were no formal rulers, and since possessions were not valued, there was little by way of rich or poor. To be sure, there were some who were improvident, and there were some whose strength, wisdom, or toolmaking skills earned them respect, but compared to the civilizations that followed, foragers were egalitarian.[16]

This changed dramatically with the rise of states and empires. The emergent elites quickly tried to separate their subjects from the foragers, making clear in myth and practice the distinction between the wild and domestic in the bargain. Hunting became one of the principle ways in which the elites demonstrated their superiority over their subjects: the elites could protect them from the heathens and wild beasts that threatened their flocks and crops. Despite the fact that these early states and empires came and went, stratification as a central feature of civilization remained a constant, down to our present era. For much of this history, hunting was a consistent marker of status. Despite the persistence of stratification and the elites' domination of hunting, however, protests were irrepressible. The work of the peasants was onerous, and promises of a glorious afterlife would wear thin. Perhaps more important, the elites could not sustain their capacities to meet the needs of their subjects. These new regimes were predicated on harnessing nature in unprecedented ways, and nature proved to be an inconstant ally. Irrigation brought salination, especially in arid climates, and crop failures.[17] Nature also brought drought, plagues of locusts that ruined a year's yield, floods, and as sedentary populations grew, plagues of a viral sort leveled empires. The Black Plague (1347–1353), for example, is estimated to have killed one-third of the population of what is now western Europe. Smallpox, brought to the Western Hemisphere by Europeans, is now thought to have caused an even more catastrophic decimation of native populations, with deaths of up to 90 percent of the Indigenous populations of North and South America.[18]

Whether from crop failures, invasions, or disease, the history of civilization has scarcely been linear, and the same is true for the history of hunting. As we will see, the flux of the dominance of empires has produced quite different hunting regimes in our own time—ranging from prohibition to broad but regulated access. Critiques of hunting have become more sophisticated, and as we will see, the number of hunters has been in rather steep decline worldwide for the past forty years. This decline in hunters has coincided with a resurgence of wildlife that has posed unanticipated challenges and exposed hunting to intense scrutiny. As we grapple with our relationship to the wild, hunting has emerged as central to the debate. The debate began long ago; we'll start at the beginning. In chapter 2, we explore hunting in the Stone Age, and how, beginning some ten thousand years age, the spread of agriculture led to the emergence of empires and attempts by the elites to monopolize hunting. In chapters 3 and 4, we look at the democratization of hunting in the American colonies, and how it decimated and then, in the twentieth century, saved most game animals from extinction. Chapter 5 examines how western European and several postcolonial societies have managed wildlife and hunting, and how for all the differences in history and circumstances, we are all now contending with the difficulties of living with abundant wildlife, even as many nongame species are disappearing or on the endangered species list. Finally, in chapter 6, we discuss the prospects for hunting in the twenty-first century.

THE HUNTING PERPLEX

Killing, Ambivalence, and Dominance

Though there is still dispute about the origins of human hunting, it seems likely that our early ancestors were at least as often prey as they were predator. It is also likely that their early targets were small mammals, birds, and fish—prey that were not capable of turning the tables, as larger mammals could. Moreover, preying on large mammals would have brought early hunters into direct competition with much more powerful, fast, and adept predators. Author Barbara Ehrenreich makes a compelling case that what set us on our path to venerate those who were able to fight was our humble beginning as scavengers.[1] Following a parade of large and smaller carnivores, and inserting ourselves into the feast before the beetles and bugs cleaned things up, was an ignominious start, but a start nonetheless.

Lacking the strong jaws needed for cracking bones to get to marrow, some ancestors figured out how to use a rock to crack bones, and over millennia the stones were shaped into more efficient bone crackers. Obsidian and flints were shaped into scrapers, knives, and spearheads. Along the way, around five hundred thousand years ago, *Homo erectus* domesticated fire, which made both meat and vegetation more palatable, and crucially, more easily digestible, thus yielding greater caloric intake.

As primatologist Richard Wrangham persuasively shows, more calories made larger brains possible.[2] With larger brains came the capacity for coordinating strategies and devising better tools, all of which combined to make up for our physical disadvantages over the dominant predators of the day. Fire also was put to use modifying the landscape to encourage vegetation that was edible either for our early *Homo* precursors and/or animals on which to prey.

Our ancestors slowly worked their way toward the top of the food chain. It took a long time for fully modern humans (*Homo sapiens sapiens*) to establish themselves, but between 150,000 and 200,000 years ago, our direct ancestors began to hold their own with large predators and large game as well as overwhelm other closely related hominids, most notably the Neanderthals, who had successfully established themselves thousands of years before our direct ancestors arrived on the planet. The contact was obviously not marked by an exchange of high fives, but DNA has established that their encounters were not always hostile. Many of us have traces of Neanderthal DNA.

The conventional narrative regarding our hunter-gatherer ancestors was established several thousand years ago, when complex civilizations started to emerge. The contrast between small bands of hunter-gatherers and their more sedentary fellow humans grew large, and the differences became invidious. Hunter-gatherers were regarded as primitive savages. But what is now clear is that they were remarkably successful.[3]

Hunting and gathering was *the* mode of existence our species depended on for most of our time on earth. Indeed, against all odds, remnant pockets of hunter-gatherers have persisted down to the present: !Kung in several southern African countries, most notably in Botswana and Namibia; a number of tribes in the Amazon rain forest; Sentinalese on the Andaman Islands off the coast of India; Aboriginals in the Australian outback; and various tribal peoples in the circumpolar regions in the Western Hemisphere as well as northern Europe and Eurasia.

Hunter-gatherers moved seasonally to follow the migration of animals and available vegetation. Nomadism required traveling light. Instead of hauling possessions, they were able to fashion tools and other necessities from materials readily available along their migration paths. They were resourceful, and possessed a wealth of

Hunting and gathering was *the* mode of existence our species depended on for most of our time on earth.

knowledge about the properties of the flora and behavior of the fauna in their territories. Though most were mobile, anthropologist James C. Scott makes it clear that in fertile wetlands and estuaries, hunter-gathers established more permanent settlements and even began to cultivate food crops, creating a mixed economy that proved quite stable long before the rise of more complex civilizations.[4] Indeed, the historic wildfires in Australia in 2019 and 2020 have revealed unambiguous evidence of irrigation for "farming" thirty to forty thousand years ago, much earlier than the rise of the domestication of cereal crops in the Middle East.

These people lived simply, but were not by any means "simple." It is worth quoting at some length historian Malcolm Margolin's description of the subsistence activities of a coastal California native tribe chronicled in the journals of naval officer Jean François de la Perouse in 1786. Margolin writes,

> The Indian . . . is seen gathering acorns from an oak tree, taking what nature offers freely, all without apparent effort or advanced skill. Yet the use of acorns is anything but simple. It involves many hard-to-master and often elaborate technologies, such as making specialized baskets . . . , storing the acorns in specially constructed caches, drying, shelling, leaching, pounding, sifting, and cooking. . . . In fact,

if the entire process is measured carefully, it may take less work and certainly far less skill to create a loaf of wheat bread than a loaf of acorn bread.

Similarly, those who herd domesticated animals often envision hunting as a primitive activity, wherein the hunter goes into the woods, bags an animal, brings it home, throws it onto a fire, and eats it. What could be more "basic"? Yet the image of simplicity does not hold up under scrutiny. Deer hunting, to use one example, involved not only a high degree of skill, knowledge, and well-crafted tools, but it also entailed levels of religious and social complexity that we are only recently beginning to appreciate. The Indian hunter often underwent an extended period of preparation that included praying, sexual abstinence, dietary restrictions, dreaming and other techniques to sharpen the mind, focus the body, and ready his spirit.[5]

The details of hunter-gatherers' adaptations vary over time and across continents. Plains and coastal California Indians had different subsistence strategies, and their strategies were not the same as the !Kung of the Kalahari or Inuit, but it would not be stretching things too much to suggest that for all the differences, they would recognize likeness as readily as difference. Intriguingly in this regard, the internet has enabled hunter-gatherers across the globe to connect with one another and forge a presence in a variety of nongovernmental organizations in the United Nations to defend their interests.[6]

Yet despite such appreciations for the complexity of hunter-gatherers' know-how, the notion that they were "primitive savages" has persisted. They have been depicted as preoccupied with survival and scuffling through the bush in constant search for food. Early missionary contact with Indigenous peoples, however, began to alter this account of ignorance and privation. The rise of anthropology in the late nineteenth century added mounting evidence challenging the dominant disparagement. The reappraisal was accelerated by the paradigm-changing work of cultural anthropologist Marshall Sahlins.[7] Synthesizing a growing body of anthropological fieldwork among hunter-gatherers across the globe, Sahlins offered a counterintuitive interpretation: hunter-gatherers worked roughly four to five hours per day on average. Like Margolin, Sahlins described economic strategies that reliably met modest and largely stable needs, which could be met leaving plenty of time for rest, relaxation, and storytelling—in effect, the creation of culture. Hunter-gatherers acquired intimate knowledge of the medicinal properties of plants, and developed ever-more sophisticated use of tools and weapons. Of course there were lean times; birth rates were low, and infant mortality was high. (Abandonment was one way of staying within the limits of the number of people the band could sustain.) Sahlins was not depicting a utopian society or philosopher Jean-Jacques Rousseau's "noble savages." He was portraying a strategy and economy that was adaptive and sustainable. The question is, Why should this matter to us?

The depictions of the hunter-gatherers are among the factors that have shaped how we struggle to understand ourselves in much the same light as the current rage for DNA testing for our ancestral roots meets a need to know "where we came from." Naming our earliest direct ancestors *hunter*-gatherers fit a convenient trope that explicitly favored male dominance as the key to our evolution as a species. We now know quite certainly that hunting played a small part in the *economy*. Gathering birds' eggs, edible plants, fruits, and nuts along with capturing small mammals yielded the bulk of the band's food. Though Sahlins and others continued to use the term "hunter-gatherers," Scott suggests that it would be far more accurate to describe our ancestors as "foragers." It's arguably the case that the calories expended in a hunt exceeded those added to the band's diet. Moreover, hunting, unlike foraging, which was pretty much a daily activity, was episodic. Weeks would go by between hunts. Indeed, it seems highly probable that hunting wasn't driven by necessity. Why then did foragers hunt? If hunting contributed modestly to the diets of our distant ancestors, why did hunting occasion so much symbolic importance?

Hunting, unlike foraging, which was pretty much a daily activity, was episodic.

Like so many things about our species' prehistory, we will probably never know the full answer to these questions, but if we may follow the insight of pioneering nineteenth-century geologist Charles Lyell (1797–1875), the present may be a key to our past. Lyell reasoned that the observed process of erosion, particularly the *pace* of this geological process, had to mean that the canyons and cliffs that exist had been created by the effects of wind, water, and ice over a lengthy time, much longer than the then-prevailing view that the earth was created a mere five thousand or so years earlier. Using the same logic, can we say that foragers hunted for the same reasons some people are drawn to hunting today?

Consider the possibility that foragers viewed meat as special, as a tasty break from their daily fare. After all, there is no evidence that males did nothing but hunt. Snaring birds and small mammals was probably routine, done by young children as well as adult men and women. Hunting was distinct from foraging, governed by the movements of game and by elders or seers who intuited that it was time for a hunt.[8] Often, as Margolin and many others have reported, the decision to hunt ushered in a period of ritual preparation. Of course the specific practices varied widely, but they included separating from the band for a period of time, use of hallucinogens, sexual abstinence, special foods, and body painting. Given that there is plenty of evidence that they possessed the empirical knowledge of the animals' habits along with legendary abilities to read signs of and track their prey, why all of this fuss? Part of the answer lies in the fact that success was never assured, and risks were involved; instead of cornering an antelope, you might be stalked by a lion. The rituals no doubt steeled their resolve. It also was the occasion for rites of passage, the transition from child to adult.

Meat was a treat. Hunting for meat was exciting too—a break from ordinary activities. We are not sure that foragers found hunting "fun," but our guess is that the challenges to wit, physical exertion, and adrenalin rush that contemporary hunters report when a game animal is encountered must have been among the reasons foragers hunted. It's hard to imagine the same mix of stimulations derived from foraging. This is not to denigrate foraging of course; recall Margolin's description of all that went into gathering acorns and making them edible. Think of weaving watertight baskets, or knowing which mushrooms are edible, which will transport you to other realms, and which will kill you. There's nothing simple here—but, and it's a big but, none of these essential skills and knowledge can fairly be described as exciting. One other factor that feminist anthropology eventually brought to light is that many of these skills and knowledge streams were the invention as well as chief occupation of the women among the hunter-forager peoples. For example, author Virginia Postrel makes the case that the development of textiles was a crucial step in our species survival and success.[9]

Might the cave paintings in Lascaux, France, stone art in the Southwest of the United States, or more recently discovered cave paintings in Indonesia, reportedly the oldest known, depicting wild animals and humans (some with animal heads) be regarded as "trophies," tributes to the successful hunter(s)?[10] It is hard to be certain what these cave artists believed themselves to be doing, but archaeologists Carolyn Boyd and Kim Cox make a compelling case that the paintings in the Southwest were complex representations of beliefs about origins and the relationships of humans to the natural world. What we do know for sure is that foragers had time on their hands for what we might call leisure—for painting on a cave wall or decorating a basket with differently dyed reeds—and along the way developing explanations of how the world was created and why one's own band was better than the band across the river. It is hard not to at least entertain the proposition that hunting had a symbolic meaning that vastly exceeded the caloric contribution it made to the band. Could it be that hunting, because it involved killing, was symbolically loaded?

Hunting involves a mix of passions that in daily life would be disruptive. The chase is exciting. The consistently successful hunter would be looked up to by their band. But killing a warm-blooded animal was not to be taken lightly

Killing a warm-blooded animal was not to be taken lightly by either the hunter or the band with whom they lived.

by either the hunter or the band with whom they lived. Hunting rituals marked a psychological break from the norms of daily life, granting permission for behavior that might otherwise be unacceptable. A modern analog might be how individuals are trained for the armed forces. Basic training separates recruits from civil society, and with haircuts and the surrender of civilian clothes, close-order drills, and a thoroughly regimented routine, soldiers are created who—at least in theory—can act in ways that make killing other human beings acceptable and even honorable.

Hunter-gatherers would attest that their guilt was rendered honorable by additional rituals, most important by those involving thanking the animal for volunteering the gift of being killed. In this context, killing was understood as a reciprocal relationship—a gift, *not* a theft.[11] The hunters were welcomed back to the band with praise and a collective sharing of the hunt. They were welcomed back to "civilian" life, reassuring one and all that the bloodlust of the hunt ended on return, whether successful or not.

Though the circumstances could not be more different, we think it is fair to say that contemporary hunters contend with the same cascade of conflicting emotions on killing an animal that was faced by our hunter-gatherer forebears. And it is clear that many of today's nonhunters worry about the character of hunters, just as they did thousands of years ago. Hunting for food was and remains different from picking fruit from a tree, or digging cassava or potatoes from the earth. Present-day anxieties about hunting and hunters are rooted in the development of moral sensibilities, which have accompanied our long march to the top of the food chain. Sahlins and others have shown, as already mentioned, that hunters contributed little to the daily caloric intake of their bands. They were fully capable of meeting their nutritional needs by the undramatic and morally unproblematic activities of gathering. Hunters hunted for the challenge, excitement of the chase, and confrontation with a large animal determined to escape. And that raised—and continues to do so—the troubling question, What kind of person would enjoy killing and how will they behave on returning home?

The success of the early hunter-gatherer bands gradually led to the dispersal of modern humans out of Africa. By thirteen to eighteen thousand years ago, our direct ancestors were present on every continent except Antarctica as well as most habitable islands across the globe. Shortly after humans arrived in a new territory, large birds and animals began disappearing. Mastodons, mammoths, and other megafauna disappeared in northern Europe. Large flightless birds and large marsupials disappeared from Australia. In North America, the mammoths, giant beavers, sloths, and other large carnivores vanished within a thousand years, plus or minus, of the arrival of the "paleo-Indians," migrants from northern Asia.[12]

This pulse of what has become known as Pleistocene extinctions was initially attributed to a combination of disease and climate change. (The glaciers that had blanketed the northern hemisphere were in retreat, and the climate was changing.) The idea that the arrival of humans—who were few in number and "primitive"—could have been a factor, much less responsible for, the extinction pulse was out of the question. How could these primitives be a match for the mammoths, saber-toothed tigers, and bears as big or bigger than polar bears, to name only a few of the megafauna that roamed North America ten thousand years ago? Niles Eldredge, the notable paleontologist, helped unravel the mystery. On one of his many trips to study and catalog species in Africa, he noted that he could approach the water buffalo, elands, and other large mammals in the Land Rover he was riding in, but as soon as he or others in his group got out of the car, the animals fled. Four wheels were no big deal but two legs were a clear sign of danger. The megafauna of Africa coevolved with humans and knew to avoid them if possible.

By contrast, the megafauna of North America, Europe, and Australia had no experience with puny two-leggeds and had no reason to fear them. Hunters could approach a beast to get close enough to thrust a spear into the animal's gut and flee to a safe distance. Within a couple of days, septicemia would weaken the stricken animal and the hunters could move in for the kill. Climate change might have helped the hunters by making the large animals more accessible. We will probably never know the fine-grained details, but we do know that large animals disappeared within a thousand years of the arrival of humans.[13]

This is but one more revision of our understanding of hunter-gatherers: first their primitivism, and then their model as exemplars of living lightly on the land. In *The Ecological Indian: Myth and History*, anthropologist Shepard Krech III challenged the myth of hunter-gatherers living in harmony with nature.[14] He described hunting practices that clearly killed more animals, especially bison, than could be consumed. Krech noted that the Plains Indians had a use for virtually all of a bison, but not necessarily all the bison they killed in a given stampede. They modified their environment to suit their needs too. They used fire not only to precipitate a stampede but also to encourage fresh growth of the prairie grasses that attracted the bison and kept an otherwise encroaching forest at bay. It is possible that if left to their own devices, the natives of North America would have driven the bison to the brink, if not over the brink, of extinction. We'll never know, but the lesson of the mammoth can't be ignored. It would have taken longer than it took the descendants of migrants from England and the European continent to drive the bison to the edge, but it bears repeating that simple though their needs were, hunter-gatherers' impact on flora and fauna appears to have been far from negligible.

The development of domestication, which started with fire, began to change everything, though the full effects took thousands of years to be fully realized. There is still much that we don't know about the process, but it is clear that hunter-gatherers did not remain passive acceptors of what nature provided. They were as active as we are in modifying the environment to make things easier. For a long stretch of time, their modifications were minimal and impermanent. Yet we now confidently know that well before the full flourishing of agriculture (the so-called Neolithic Revolution, which marked the large-scale transition from foraging to agrarianism), various hunter-forager cultures on several continents had already added the domestication of plants to their subsistence strategies. As journalist Charles C. Mann, Scott, and writer Bruce Pascoe demonstrate, hunter-gatherers had begun serious manipulations of their environments that foreshadowed what was to come.[15] What came, with fits and starts, was ultimately transformative, but before we get to the full domestication of plants and *some* animals, let's briefly consider the messy transition.

As we would expect of ourselves, hunter-gatherers improved their technology and techniques. For those groups lucky enough to claim turf in areas where annual flooding left deposits of fertile soil that created a rich, varied food source for humans and wildlife, hunter-gatherers could set up more or less permanent settlements. It's probably not an accident that the Okavango Valley in southern Africa is regarded as our species' birthplace.[16] Here nomadic groups could settle down, if not for a full year, at least long enough to establish trade relations with people as far away as the eastern coast of Africa. Archaeologists have uncovered middens revealing shells of mollusks and bones of fish that had to originate far from the valley.[17] Unlike earlier hunter-gatherers who left few traces in the archaeological record, these people left signatures that allow insight into the variety of foods they ate as well as traces that they harvested grains that volunteered from their "dumps" at the edge of the places where they set up their temporary "camps." These semisedentary groups appeared before domestication, most likely in floodplains that were dependably, naturally fertile. They lived in small groups, and still practiced the time-tested strategies of hunting and gathering, yet there is also evidence of the use of grains that predates known domestication. For example, Pascoe reports that millstones dating to twenty-five thousand years ago have been found in Australia.

These early instances of what we might think of as "experiments" in sedentarism were not only the exception; they were precarious. By contrast, the mobile, resourceful hunter-gatherers could weather drought and floods. They could flee danger without regard for protecting possessions since they could easily fashion the tools (including baskets, woven nets, and garments) from widely available raw materials.

Roughly ten to twelve thousand years ago, people in the Fertile Crescent in and around the Tigress and Euphrates Rivers began to systematically cultivate wheat and barley. Unlike the continuing mystery about how maize became maize, the story of wheat and barley (and soon after, rice and other grains) is rather straightforward. When wheat and barley ripened in the wild, the seeds shattered, exploding away from the stem to scatter on the ground. The grain was great for mice and birds, but even a starving person would not think of crawling around collecting the tiny seeds. As luck would have it, though, some observant individuals noticed that in some plants, the seeds ripened yet did not shatter. These seeds could be easily collected, processed, and turned into nutritious food. It was only a matter of time until some unknown savant figured out that if some seeds from nonshattering plants were saved and planted, they would produce more nonshattering wheat and barley plants.

The Fertile Crescent was not the first site of plant domestication, but seems to have been the first to persist and give rise to empires. Similar domestication of plants occurred in Asia and South Asia (rice) some six to seven thousand years ago. In Peru about three thousand years ago, the people living in the highlands domesticated cotton, which they wove into nets and traded to coastal villages in exchange for fish. This may be the first verified example of the domestication of a nonfood crop.[18] Contemporary plant geneticists still can't agree on how people in southern Mexico figured out roughly six thousand years ago how to coax a plant that produced inedible kernels into a plant that has become one of the dominant staple crops that feeds millions: maize.

Before we begin to assess how this transformation changed how we lived, labored, and hunted, there are two other dimensions of domestication that need to be taken into account: the domestication of animals and water. There is still some dispute about the timing of the domestication of food crops and a relatively small number of animals. Which came first, plants or animals? We won't attempt to settle that here, though it's important for our interest in hunting to note that anthropologist Pat Shipman argues that the first animal domesticated was derived from wolves some thirty thousand years ago, becoming "man's best friend."

Shipman refers to some of our domesticated animals—dogs, cattle, horses, sheep and goats, swine, camels, and llamas, to mention the most prominent of the domesticates—as "living tools."[19] More than supplying meat (and milk, wool, and skins), they labored for us, transporting us great distances, carrying heavy loads, and of course, plowing fields. When the Spanish introduced horses to

North America, the Plains Indians quickly discovered that horses made hunting bison much more productive. (We don't want to say "easier"; it was still risky business.) Like the stone and wood tools our ancestors sculpted, the animals we domesticated had to be "sculpted," trained and ultimately bred for specific tasks, including hunting.

It probably isn't an accident that cultivation in the Fertile Crescent persisted where there was abundant water. But domesticated crops require predictable water, and it didn't take long to realize that water would have to be brought to the newly cultivated fields. If planting and harvesting were labor intensive, digging and maintaining irrigation canals was an order of magnitude more onerous.

As Scott makes clear, these "revolutions" of domestication must have puzzled most hunter-gatherers. Why trade a tried-and-true as well as relatively easy life for one that entailed steady, heavy labor? Living off the land, as opposed to laboring on the land, must have been seen by many, if not most, hunter-gatherers as far preferable. There is evidence from the analysis of the bones of hunter-gatherers and early farmers that the former were healthier than the latter.[20]

This calculus posed a serious challenge to those who were themselves *becoming domesticated* as much as they *were domesticating* nature. If the rigors of farming became onerous, and hunting and gathering remained live options, how was a labor force maintained? The answer is obvious: some form of coercion. What's not obvious is why people submitted when escape along with a return to hunting and gathering was possible. This remained a serious problem well into the modern era. Industrialist Henry Ford, despite his promise of five dollars a day, had trouble keeping his employees at his machines. Labor turnover was high; with roots still in small farms, and fish and game in some places still abundant, workers quit. The British solved this problem earlier with the Enclosure Acts, which literally forced the peasantry off the land and eventually into the textile mills. In any event, some settlements survived and produced enough surplus to support a hierarchy: a small proportion of the population that ruled the rest of the population that did the work. Whether they ruled by brute force or charisma, it's impossible to say. Historian Walter Scheidel adds to Scott's account of the gradual rise and spread of agrarian states, which we do not have to detail here, though it is important to note that the rise of states meant that hierarchy and the systematic coercion of labor became integral.[21] Suffice it to say, by six thousand years ago the die was cast, and while civilizations like Mesopotamia and Babylon came and went, domestication persisted, and in the course of five to six thousand years had spread to all continents except Antarctica. This is not to say that hunting and gathering disappeared. As we mentioned earlier, it persists in small pockets even down to the present.

As domestication took root and spread, humans' understanding of themselves in relation to nature changed. Hunter-gatherers understood themselves as a part of nature, if not exactly coequals with the flora, fauna, and geological features they lived alongside. As we began to be domesticated, we started to think that we were *apart* from nature—and not just apart but also locked in a struggle with nature. There were weeds and insects to battle, water to move, and crops and flocks to protect from predators and pesky hunter-gatherers. In effect, we drew an ever-sharper distinction between the *wild* and *domestic*, the civilized and barbarian—a distinction that continues to bedevil us to this day.

Hunting—and the reasons to hunt—changed as well. Agrarians no doubt still hunted for subsistence, but now there was a need to protect crops and flocks from wild animals. Carnivores, once admired for their cunning and hunting skills, and often incorporated into rituals of the hunt and adopted as clan totems, became loathed. Herbivores fared a bit better because they had long been seen as food, but they too could wreak havoc on a ripening crop of grain. Killing animals that threatened domestic animals or crops became just another task—not that much different from weeding, planting, and harvesting. Regarding wild animals as pests—as threats to crops, domestic flocks, and well-being—changed the farmer's and pastoralist's relationship to wildlife.

It's hard to say with any precision when the elites—that small slice of a state's population that lived off the labors of those who tilled the soil, dug the irrigation canals, and tended the "living tools," began to arrogate unto themselves exclusive rights to hunt (as opposed to killing pests). Yet we know from Greek, Roman, and Hindu myths that hunting became a signifier of status and power. (Recall Xenophon's annual garden celebration of the goddess of the hunt.) And the monopolization of the hunt meant that the peasants would remain tied to the tilling of the fields and digging of irrigation channels. We cannot possibly do justice to the wide variations in hunting across the cultures that arose with the spread of agriculture, much less to all the variations that unfolded over the course of roughly 6000 BCE to the late nineteenth century, but we can briefly examine the core features of how the rise of empires and ultimately nation-states shaped hunting.

Hunting quite probably became the first sport of kings. Historian Erich Hobusch's survey of the history of hunting documents how kings and emperors carved out exclusive hunting grounds for themselves, and were prepared to punish, sometimes harshly, interlopers.[22] Varying degrees of monopolization by elites appear almost as soon as stable regimes arise across the Middle East, Eurasia, South Asia, and Europe. Unfortunately the traces of the ancient world are biased in favor of those elites whose possessions, burial sites, palaces, and temples are far more likely to have survived as evidence as compared to the modest belongings of the peasants. As a result, we cannot be sure how complete the elite domination of hunting was in the earliest empires or how commoners hunted. Commoners must have hunted and at least occasionally risked hunting on private reserves. In some regions, the domination of hunting by elites became nearly complete for periods of time. England was one such extreme example. In 1723, in response to a rise in poaching, the Black Act was passed, making poaching a capital crime. (The law was repealed in 1823.)

Another common feature of hunting in the emerging empires was a focus on killing top carnivores and other dangerous animals. The Assyrian king Tiglath-Pilser I (1112–1074 BCE) boasted, "On the order of Ninurta, my patron, I have, with a brave heart, killed 120 lions in a terrible fight, facing animals on foot. I have also killed 800 lions from my war chariot."[23] Classical archaeologist Judith Barringer reports that confrontations with wild boar were common in depictions of the hunt in ancient Greece.[24] The Romans notoriously made spectacles of combat with lions. In India, the elite hunters proved themselves by killing tigers and leopards, especially doing so in direct hand-to-claw confrontations.[25] Dangerous animals provided a test of valor and strength that lent the elites an aura of invincibility as well as superhuman capacities. The elites' ability to dominate the wildest beasts made their dominance over their subjects seem legitimate. It also underscored the claim that the elites were capable of protecting the weak.

Piling up the carcasses of large, dangerous animals must have been impressive. But it wasn't enough for some. The same king of Assyria who boasted of killing hundreds of lions added, almost as an afterthought, "All kind of game of the fields and fowls in the sky I made my quarry."[26] Over time these royal hunts became more and more elaborate, enlisting hundreds of peasants to drive game, large and small, to the waiting hunters. As with so much of what we've discussed, practices of distributing the meat varied widely and details are scarce. It's admittedly a guess, yet it seems likely that in the earliest stages of state formation, sharing the bounty was probably common, but in mature states, where stratification was explicit and rigid, and where the royals were surrounded by a large retinue of courtiers, little, if anything, would trickle down to the peasantry.

The Assyrian king's boast reveals another feature of the postforager era: the melding of hunting and warfare. Foragers must have faced conflicts that occasioned violence, either within the band or between neighboring ones. But the ethnographic details of foraging groups indicate that while some were indeed "warlike," the vast majority of the ethnographies of hunter-gatherers record low levels of intra- and intergroup conflict.[27] Apart from the human condition of thin skins, foragers had little to fight over. There was little inequality, there was episodic scarcity, and the norm of sharing was strongly buttressed by the group.[28]

The rise of states and empires quickly changed group and intergroup behaviors. The blending of hunting and combat in these early states made perfect sense. For reasons we've alluded to, the early states required a labor force to generate the surplus that allowed a handful of people to rule. This imposed serious constraints that hunter-gatherers largely avoided: the surplus needed to be protected from wild animals and raids from other states, and the need to maintain a labor force led to forays to capture and enslave as well as prevent laborers from fleeing the fields to return to the freer life of foraging. This required what quickly became the beginnings of a formal, trained cadre capable of protecting the settlement from external threats, internal disruptions, and escapes, and having the capacity to project force should the need arise. The skills, weapons, and tactics that hunters had developed over millennia for the hunt were easily transferable to the state's defense.

As significant as the weapons and tactics were, the rituals that prepared men to hunt animals could easily be transformed into preparations for battle. Barringer makes it clear that in ancient Greece, the initiation rites of at least the sons of citizens explicitly linked hunting to preparation for combat. Thus began a symbiotic relationship between hunters and warriors. To be sure, it probably never was the case that all hunters were soldiers, or all soldiers were hunters, though they may have started out hunting. As we will see in the following chapters, however, weapons used for hunting became weapons of war, and weapons of war, which tended to be continually improved, found their way into the forests and fields, with the Assyrian king in his war chariot leading the way.

It would be a mistake, though, to assume that this link meant that hunting and combat were interchangeable, or that hunters and soldiers were or are interchangeable. The formal discipline and hierarchy required of a soldier bears almost no resemblance to how a hunter behaves. States quickly created what today would be regarded as a "standing army" made up of palace guards, overseers, and sheriffs, all fitted into the growing hierarchy of royals, priests, and courtiers—and don't forget tax collectors. This said, it is important to acknowledge that the association of warfare and hunting no doubt added to concerns about the character of people associated in one way or another with violence.

The final feature of how the rise of states affected hunting no doubt flows from this concern about character and violence. It is not stretching things to say that the rise of civilizations codified complex myths to justify and, crucially, set conditions for the legitimacy of killing. From the

Greeks we got Artemis, the goddess of the hunt and wild animals; from the Romans came Diana, the counterpoint to Artemis; and India contributed Banka-Murdi, the goddess of the hunt and fertility. From Africa to South America to Europe and the Far East, gods and goddesses were sought to bless the hunt. The object was to ensure success, but the gods of course work in mysterious ways; success can be elusive. This indeterminacy no doubt sparked efforts to explain why the gods either looked with favor on the hunters or did not. The explanations varied over time and place, but everywhere versions of what was proper versus transgressive in hunting emerged and became codified. Much was indebted to the rituals and beliefs that foragers had generated as well as passed along in vibrant oral traditions. As we will see in the chapters ahead, hunting (and hunters) continued to face suspicion and critiques. The response was in effect an evolution in justifications of hunting, but the justifications were required by questions that dogged our early ancestors as much as they shape our own struggles with the legitimacy of hunting.

There are various places to dig for these justifications, but we will begin where our cultural history tells us to: the ancient world of Greece and Rome. The myths and rituals of ancient Greece portray the central role that hunter awareness played in the understanding of culture, at large and in relationship to nature. The historian Xenophon (fifth to fourth century BCE) maintained a hunting ground on his estate near Sparta, complete with a temple to Artemis. There he held an annual festival in honor of the goddess of the hunt:

> All citizens and neighbors, both men and women, took part in the festival. The goddess provided barley, wheat bread, wine, dried fruits, and a portion of the sacrifices from the holy pasture, and from the hunted animals too. For a hunt was held at the festival by Xenophon's sons and those of the other citizens, and any of the grown men who wished to also took part. They took game, some from the holy ground itself and some from Pholoe, boars and roe deer and fallow deer. This festival was a community celebration of shared values that went beyond mere recreation, nourishment, or thanksgiving. Like many of his contemporaries, Xenophon believed that hunting was both an inducement to and a mark of moral rectitude. In his *Cynegeticus* (usually translated as "On Hunting" or "Hunting with Dogs"), he argued that "to be taught what is good by one's own nature is best of all," and that natural lesson is nowhere better observed than in various forms of hunting. Significantly, in an age when women's social sphere was sharply segregated from the world of men, Xenophon objected, "[W]hat has sex to do with it? It is not only men enamored of the chase that have

become heroes, but among women there are also to whom our lady Artemis has granted a like boon—Atalanta, and Procris, and many another huntress fair."[29]

"To be taught what is good by one's own nature is best of all." But unlike the rarefied "know thyself" of Artemis's twin brother, Apollo, the lessons imparted by the shaft-showering goddess were bought at the expense of getting dirt and blood under one's fingernails. Artemis—the Lady of the Wild Things—was simultaneously the goddess of hunting and childbirth, both protector and slayer of young, vulnerable life. This Maiden of the Crescent Moon, who cheerily engaged in a celestial round dance with her companion nymphs, was at the same time She Who Slays, a dark goddess who demanded animal and human sacrifice. As any of the guests at Xenophon's big backyard barbecue would have been the first to acknowledge, you wouldn't want to get on the wrong side of her!

Artemis was wildness and wilderness itself, but wildness of a particular sort. Agrotera, one of Artemis's primary titles, meant not simply the "outside world" as "outdoors" but more specifically the "world outside the city walls." That is to say, hers is the kind of wildness that exists in necessary tension with civilization. She is always just outside the boundary, across the border, over the edge.

Figure 7

Of course, hunters understand that intrinsic to the idea of boundaries is their permeability. They exist to be inhabited, crossed over. Dawn and dusk, the boundary times between night and day, are the best times for hunting. The best places are those edges or ecotones where one kind of habitat gives way to another, where differences and distinctions inevitably blur. Hunting those edges, one discerns that in its workings, the world is far more complex and subtle than the (Apollonian) intellect's too-facile distinctions seek to make it: domestic/wild, human/animal, culture/nature, rationality/instinct, male/female, and life/death. Ultimately what one learns "by one's own nature" is the lesson not simply of one's own mortality but more important one's participation in the life/death/life cycle of the natural world.

The myths and pageantry of elite hunting served the elites well, but they couldn't quell criticism. Two examples of this will have to suffice to illustrate the long-term fragility of elite hunting; both involve Great Britain and its empire. The Puritan and Quaker opposition to the Crown focused on the excesses of the elites, not least of which were their extravagant hunts, which offended the sensibilities of the Protestant sects for which excess was the equivalent of idolatry. When the dissenters established the American colonies, they established the foundations of what would become, through twists and turns, a democratic model of hunting, sharply juxtaposed to the elite one.

A continent away in India, and a century and a half later, the British, who by then had responded to discontent at home by elaborating a hunting ethos that became the "sporting hunter," celebrated the chase and rejected the goal of piling up mountains of dead animals (or at least the celebration and public display of such accomplishments). But they conceded to the local Indian elites, who depended on extravagant hunts to affirm their status.[30] When India won independence in 1947, the new government essentially outlawed almost all hunting.

The legacy of the centuries-long elite domination of hunting has created three different hunting cultures. One, dominant in some former colonies, is a flat-out ban on hunting (to be discussed in chapter 5); second is an elite sporting tradition, followed in much of Europe and the British Isles; and third is a democratic model of hunting that has characterized North America. We turn next to North America.

THE DEMOCRATIZATION OF THE HUNT IN NORTH AMERICA

The English colonists who boarded the *Mayflower* to seek their religious freedom and fortunes in the "new world" brought with them an abiding dislike of aristocracy. The reasons for this were many, among them a critique of game laws that restricted access to hunting for the commoners and levied harsh penalties for poaching. The Puritans were ambivalent about hunting, but they were not equivocal about aristocratic privilege, and were disgusted by the extravagance and excesses of the royal hunts.

The problem with hunting was twofold from the Puritans' perspective. First and perhaps foremost, hunting excited passions that distracted from gainful work and prayerfulness. Though Pilgrims have an unearned reputation for being killjoys, it is true that they saw North America as an ungodly wilderness (Plymouth governor William Bradford famously called it "a howling wilderness") that they were obliged by God to domesticate. That meant clearing forests, tilling fields, and building fences and walls to mark private property as well as confine domestic animals. Second—and a close second at that—was the problem we discussed in the previous chapter: if hunting is a viable strategy for survival, the grip of the community over individuals is loosened. If someone found the demands of piety and hard work too onerous, exit was all too tempting.

The Puritans landed in fall 1620 on Cape Cod. It's unclear if they brought domestic animals with them, but if they did, space would have precluded large domesticates. They must have depended on fish, birds, small game (rabbits), and an occasional deer (most of which would have retreated into deeper woods to ride out the New England winter). Spring must have felt like deliverance—proof of God's wisdom. The rivers and streams teemed with salmon, herring, eels, and shad. Ducks, geese, swans, and passenger pigeons came in waves, heading for spring breeding grounds. In the absence of crops and cattle, the colony was heavily dependent on hunting and fishing for survival.

With food assured, they set about clearing land for planting along with building shelters and a house of worship. All hands were on deck to do God's work. The colony survived, with some assistance from the local Wampanoag (who brought several deer to the "first Thanksgiving" to add to the fowl the Puritans had shot in fall 1621). As fields were cleared and planted, and ships from England began arriving with cattle and more colonists, hunting took on a decidedly commercial edge. Meat (especially venison), deer hides, and furs (particularly beaver pelts) were highly prized in England, and along with fish (salt cod) and timber, became major exports from the Massachusetts Bay Colony.

The importance of hunting at least partially relieved any moral ambivalence that the Puritans harbored. But hunting gave rise to conflicts that are familiar to us. One conflict arose from concerns over safety. Early on laws were passed forbidding the discharge of guns across public ways, and too close to dwellings and outbuildings (barns, stables, and the like). Another major conflict was, in economics professor James Tober's words, over "who owns the wildlife."[1]

In the New England colonies, most towns established commons—areas owned by the residents in common where they could gather for public events, graze livestock, and so on. Most land, however, was privately held. The question of ownership of wildlife naturally arose, such as, Do the deer browsing in my woodlot belong to me? Of course, there was little dispute about who owned domestic animals, but wild animals were a different thing altogether. Not only that, though the Puritans did not dispute the principle of private property, the resentment of aristocratic privilege inclined them to assert that wild animals were held in common. The fact that at any moment in time, a deer or turkey was on my property did not make it mine since ten minutes from now, it might be on my neighbor's property. Tober makes it clear that the Puritans resolved this question in favor of regarding wild animals as common property. Indeed, that gave rise to the legalistic definition of a wild animal that has been killed: it was "reduced to possession."

That leaves but one challenge hunting posed to the intensely community-oriented Puritans: keeping people committed to the community along with its demands for labor and piety, and not being lured away by the ease with which one could live off the land. In this regard, consider Thomas Morton. Morton left England to visit the new colony briefly in 1622 and liked what he saw—not the settlement (he bridled at all the rules), but the abundant commercial opportunities nature offered. He returned with a small group of like-minded fellows and set up camp a few miles from the Puritans' settlement at Plymouth. In short order, Morton struck up a relationship with the Wampanoags, and started a brisk trade for profitable hides and beaver pelts, which were used to fashion popular hats for men and women in England. Morton and his followers thrived. Bradford and the leaders of Plymouth objected to Morton's trading with the natives. In 1628, Plymouth militia commander Myles Standish led a group of men and arrested Morton, who was then tried and convicted of selling arms to the natives. He was banished to a desolate island off the coast awaiting deportation to England. A year later, the village that Morton founded was sacked and burned to the ground.[2]

The lesson was stark, but with new arrivals from England, many drawn, like Morton, by tales of abundant land and game more than by devotion to Puritan theocracy, the die was cast. Plymouth didn't collapse—far from it. It flourished and left an indelible stamp on American culture. Yet the fact that it was easy to do what Morton had done, though not necessarily with Morton's flair, meant that many newcomers established their own settlements, not all of them modeled on Puritan orthodoxy. There was game aplenty, free for the taking, and a robust market for the fruits of the hunt. The forests provided building materials, and there was a market for lumber, both in England and domestically as the population in cities grew. In other words, the risks of exit were low, and for new arrivals, the benefits of association grew less and less compelling as settlements that were doctrinally more "liberal" became more numerous. The Puritans, for all of their ambivalence about hunting, had to settle for a ban on hunting on Sundays (the only "blue law" restrictions on commercial and most other secular activities on the Sabbath, still in force in Massachusetts and Maine).

Thus hunting came to be regarded as a right. This is not to say that everyone hunted. So far as we can tell, there is no reliable estimate of the percentage of the population in the New England colonies that hunted (and/or trapped). Still, given the speed with which land was cleared and stone walls were built to mark property boundaries, serious hunters—hunters whose livelihoods depended on hunting for the market—must have been a distinct minority. It is likely that many men and some women hunted at some point, however, mostly when they were teenagers and young adults.

It also should be noted before we proceed that early on, the colonists depended heavily, as had Morton, on native hunting and trapping skills. By definition, given the prohibitions on hunting the king's game, the colonists' skills were, shall we say, undeveloped. And as already mentioned, the Puritans were ambivalent about hunting. As historian Daniel Justin Herman observes, quoting Bradford, "'For us to seek for deer it doth not boot [profit],' explained Plymouth Governor William Bradford, because Indians could kill game more efficiently than colonists could."[3] It was better for the colonists to apply themselves to clearing land, planting crops, and relying on domestic animals for their meat.

Additionally, the colonists' muskets were not all that accurate or reliable. The natives may have been impressed by the noise and smoke of a musket's discharge, but the net result could easily be bested by a native archer. Moreover, hunting involves much more than shooting straight. The successful hunter has to know the animal's habits and,

Hunting involves much more than shooting straight.

crucially, its habitat. Where is the deer or turkey likely to be at a specific time of day and season of the year, depending on the weather that particular day? This is not rocket science, to be sure, but it requires attention to details that someone new to a place, confronting unfamiliar forests, with no access to the Weather Channel, has to painstakingly acquire. As Herman points out, the Puritans actively punished those who ventured too deep into the forest, lest they become "lost souls," literally or figuratively.[4]

It's impossible to know how many of the hides, pelts, and meat the colonists sent back to England were actually acquired by trade with local Indigenous communities, yet the evidence is pretty compelling that early on, the natives contributed heavily to these exports. Indeed, conflict between native nations was sparked by natives who, having exhausted the supply of beaver on their traditional hunting/trapping grounds, moved into others' traditional hunting/trapping grounds.[5] It did not take all that long for the colonists to recognize the profits that could be made by exporting fur, hides, and flesh to England. Historian Andrea Smalley's study of hunting in the mid-Atlantic colonies shows that the export of the fruits of the hunt made up a significant share of the colonies' economies. Furthermore, the depletion of game locally became a significant spur to westward expansion in both the northern and southern colonies.

The colonists who settled in the South appeared to have had little or no ambivalence about hunting. As historian Nicolas Proctor demonstrates, southern slave owners saw hunting as integral to affirming both their masculinity and dominance over the enslaved. The plantation owners were also inclined to emulate the British aristocracy, unlike the colonists in New England. Plantation owners joined hunt clubs that promoted hunting as a manly sport, distinct from the subsistence hunting that poor whites and enslaved peoples engaged in.

Despite this popular affinity for aristocratic affects, wild game came to be regarded as "common property," as it was in the New England colonies. A court opinion in Georgia made this clear when a man was accused of shooting game on a neighbor's property. The complaint was based on the English Black Act, which the Georgia court decided in 1808 could not apply to the colony. The judge ruled that the law did not apply "because it was clearly 'founded upon a tender solicitude for the amusement and property of the aristocracy of England.' The review was 'not only penal to feudal degree . . . [but also] productive of tyranny.'" The judge went further to declare that "the liberty of killing deer . . . was as unrestrained as the natural rights of deer to rove."[6]

Proctor makes it clear that enslaved boys and their owners' sons fished and hunted together, and that these associations sometimes led to lifelong relationships, though simultaneously keeping the master-slave hierarchy intact. Few trusted slaves were allowed to borrow or own a gun, but most played supporting roles in the hunt, tending the horses and hounds. Slaves also hunted on their own, sometimes surreptitiously, using traps, slingshots, and clubs, to supplement the spartan diets afforded by their owners.[7] Although Proctor does not comment on this, the dominance of the slave owners in the southern colonies probably moderated the commercialization of the hunt that occurred in the mid-Atlantic colonies that Smalley studied as well as the New England colonies.[8]

By the mid-eighteenth century, scarcely more than a hundred years after the first settlement, turkeys had disappeared from southern New England, and deer had become so scarce in the Massachusetts Bay Colony that hunting was suspended for three years beginning in 1718. Authorities continued to periodically issue bans on the hunting of deer across the colonies throughout the century.[9] Unfortunately enforcement was, to say the least, ineffective. Timothy Dwight, a native of Northampton, Massachusetts, grandson of the notable Puritan minister Jonathan Edwards, and the eighth president of Yale University, summarized the situation in 1821: "Hunting with us . . . exists chiefly in the tales of other times."[10]

The Puritans may not have had a direct role in the depletion of game with their muskets, given their ambivalence to hunting, but they contributed mightily with their saws and axes. They attacked the forests with religious zeal, depriving wildlife of habitat. They also built dams to harness the energy of flowing water to power the mills they built to process grain and logs, and ultimately power textile mills. The combination of deforestation and dams degraded habitat for the once-abundant migrations of salmon, herring, and shad as well as the populations of native trout.[11]

As the population grew, both from a robust birth rate and steady stream of immigrants, the pressures of played-out resources combined with a growing population led inexorably to westward expansion. It began as a practical response to the desire for land and access to the as-yet-unexploited forests and fauna. But by the mid-nineteenth century, it became a secular "calling." The doctrine of Manifest Destiny was born. The idea that the United States was destined to establish dominion over what ultimately became the contiguous forty-eight states was not without opposition, but it plainly struck a chord with people restless to be free and independent.

The Homestead Act of 1862, promising 160 acres to anyone who had not taken up arms against the US government, and agreed to settle and improve the land, while not invoking Manifest Destiny per se, nevertheless gave a mighty boost to westward movement. (There were subsequent acts extending settlements ever farther westward.) The results were, sadly, predictable, and wildlife populations were decimated in the wake of advancing settlers.

However reluctant or inept the early colonists were with their muskets, the new waves of settlers had fewer qualms about hunting. More important, a revolution was taking place in the manufacture of firearms that made muskets instantly obsolete. The innovation, spurred by Eli Whitney, the inventor of the cotton gin of all things, involved manufacturing to high tolerances so that a rifle could be mass-produced using machine-interchangeable parts. Unlike the handmade musket, the rifle was easy to keep in working order and far more accurate. Significantly, rifles were also affordable. This one crucial innovation—the mass production of interchangeable parts—triggered a rapid succession of innovations that featured repeating rifles, encased bullets, and rifled barrels that further increased accuracy.

The innovations in the production of rifles were driven by political decisions beginning with the Jefferson administration to improve the defenses of the new republic. The guarantee of large orders from the federal government attracted investors and spurred innovation. At first intended for the military, it didn't take long, once the idea of mass production was vindicated, for the budding arms industry, initially located in shops along the Connecticut River Valley from New Haven north into Vermont, to begin producing guns designed for hunting. The idea of mass production based on interchangeable parts spread to the production of almost everything else—from sewing machines to automobiles—and came to be known as the "American system of manufactures." It stunned the world and launched the United States as an industrial powerhouse.[12]

The combination of a growing market for game (meat, hides, fur, and feathers), railroads connecting the hinterlands to the growing cities and ports on the East Coast, radically improved hunting firearms, and lax enforcement of a patchwork of regulations governing hunting all set the stage for what can only be called an onslaught on the nation's wildlife.

As historian Philip Dray notes, as the West became accessible, European elites began to outfit themselves for often-extravagant hunts there—sometimes lasting a year or more.[13] Having reduced many big game creatures to carefully managed numbers at home, the aristocrats could enjoy unfettered access to the still-abundant deer, antelope, bison, bears, and cougars in the United States—but not for long.

Wildlife no doubt enjoyed a respite while the Civil War raged on, yet the carnage resumed at the war's end. No species was spared, but bison were especially targeted. They traveled in huge herds—unlike deer, moose, elk, and

Wildlife no doubt enjoyed a respite while the Civil War raged on, yet the carnage resumed at the war's end.

antelope, and their hides and tongues fetched a good price. Dray cites a sample of diary entries by a member of one of the many groups of "hide men" preying on the bison:

> 1867—We save every tongue so as we would know how many we killed. . . . In all we killed 22,000.
>
> 1872—We made a camp on the Smoky and I went to killing just for the hides. It was the 22nd of September and was too warm to save any meet [*sic*]. When Charley came up I had killed 1,900 buffaloes and hauled the hides to Grinnell station.
>
> 1872—We went north about 30 miles and made camp for about 40 days. We killed 24,000 buffaloes and a number of antelopes. Then we went northwest over on the Republican. We camped at the Big Spring . . . about 30 days and killed about 800 buffaloes.[14]

Market hunting was largely responsible for the mounting decimation of wildlife. The eighteenth and nineteenth centuries were not a good time for wildlife, and given the lingering Puritan ambivalence toward hunting, it was no better for the reputation of hunters. By definition, the market hunters and "mountain men" who roamed the far west in search of beaver and hides lived on the margins of society. If they farmed at all, they did so improvidently. They were regarded as coarse and shiftless; their occupation, killing, conjured violence and savagery. Their association, though often hostile, with Indigenous communities did not improve their reputation.[15]

By the last third of the nineteenth century, it was apparent that the democratization of the hunt was quickly leading to what a century later ecologist Garret Hardin called "the tragedy of the commons."[16] With few, if any, restrictions on the taking of game, it was in no individual's interest to practice restraint, *particularly when there was money to be made*. Dwight's rueful comment on the state of hunting was an early signal that there were stirrings in the early nineteenth century that began to change the image of the hunter—or more accurately, started to disassociate hunting from what amounted to unrelenting slaughter. The hostility toward the old-world aristocracy—with the exception of the South noted—and humble origins of most of the colonists and settlers, lent a sense of egalitarianism to the new republic that gave substance to the Declaration of Independence's "All men are created equal." Of course, in reality, there was a growing number of wealthy individuals and others, merely well-to-do, who had the privilege to enjoy various leisurely diversions. Some, for whatever reasons, chose hunting and the shooting sports.

The artist, naturalist, and hunter John James Audubon (1785–1851) was among the first of these sport hunters to sense what lay in store for wildlife. He decided to devote himself to memorializing the fauna of North

America. His stunning representations of birds and mammals struck a chord that reverberated long after he died. But Audubon's critique of prevailing hunting practices was muted by his own love of hunting. He admired frontiersmen Daniel Boone, whose hunting exploits made him a US legend, and Audubon sought to hunt with him. (It is unclear whether they ever did hunt together. Boone was quite old when Audubon was a young man.)

An immigrant from England, novelist William Henry Herbert came to the United States in 1831. An aristocrat who'd fallen on hard times, Herbert brought with him a sensibility that included a disdain for market hunters and the lower-class "pot hunters"—people who hunted primarily for food. He adopted the pen name Frank Forester, and began writing articles decrying the decimation of wildlife while drawing a sharp distinction between market hunters and hunters he characterized as sportsmen. Herbert was arguably the single most influential voice for protecting wildlife in the years leading up to the Civil War.

Anticipating virtually all the elements of what would come to define sport hunting by the late nineteenth and early twentieth centuries, Herbert insisted that what separated market and sport hunting was the emphasis on "fair play" as well as the thrill of the chase that defined sport hunting. By contrast, market hunters only cared about killing. "We save every tongue so as we would know how many we killed." As Herbert put it,

It is not in the inevitable certainty of success—
for certainty destroys the excitement, which is
the soul of sport—but it is the vigor, science
[correct technique], and manhood displayed—in
the difficulties to be overcome, in the pleasurable
anxiety for success, and the uncertainty of it, . . . and
above all, in the unalterable *love of fair play*, that
first thought of the genuine sportsman, that true
sportsmanship consists.[17]

Herbert also anticipated the criticism of the heedless
destruction of wildlife habitat that would gather momentum in the years immediately following the end of the Civil
War. But it was a native Vermonter, George Perkins Marsh,
who set the stage for what came to be known as the conservation movement.[18] A native of Woodstock, he became
first a state legislator, and then was appointed by Abraham
Lincoln as the US diplomat (then the equivalent to an am-
bassador) to Turkey and later Italy. His early experience in
Vermont, where extensive logging along with the intensive
grazing of sheep and goats had denuded large portions of
the state, and his observations of how, centuries earlier,
the same had happened in the Mediterranean, led him to
conclude that humans' destructiveness had to be checked.
Marsh painstakingly chronicled how people were degrad-
ing the environment in the United States and argued for a

radical shift toward the management of natural resources based on science, not unchecked profit seeking.

Environmental historian William Cronon, in the foreword to David Lowenthal's definitive biography of Marsh, *George Perkins Marsh: Prophet of Conservation*, summarized Marsh's impact:

> Its [*Man and Nature*'s]arguments helped buttress efforts in New York State during the 1870s and 1880s to create a permanent "forest reserve" in the Adirondack Mountains. . . . The result was the creation in 1885 of Adirondack State Park, at over 700,000 acres the largest wildland park east of the Mississippi River. This in turn laid the groundwork for the passage by Congress in 1891 of the Forest Reserve Act, giving the President the power to set aside tracts of forest land at the headwaters of rivers supplying major American cities with water. The law's justification was straight out of the pages of George Perkins Marsh's book, and it created the national forests as we know them today.[19]

The times were indeed changing. A new generation, born a decade or so before the Civil War, was moved by the legacy of Audubon and Herbert, and Marsh's plea for the enlightened stewardship of the nation's natural resources.

Prominent among them were two young men who became leading figures in the mobilization of sport hunters to lead efforts to promote conservation. William Temple Hornaday (1854–1937) began his career as a taxidermist for the Smithsonian Institution (which Marsh played a crucial role in establishing), where like Audubon before him, he dedicated himself to gathering specimens of the United States' fast-disappearing wildlife. A trained zoologist, he went on to become the first director of the New York Zoological Park (now the Bronx Zoo) and arranged for the transportation of a small herd of bison to New York City to protect the species from extinction. Descendants of this captive herd were reintroduced to the West in the early twentieth century.

Hornaday was a hunter, but appalled by the destruction of wildlife, he ultimately gave up hunting and urged others to do so too. In what Dray characterized as a

strongly worded chastisement to Congress and the nation, *Our Vanishing Wildlife: Its Extermination and Preservation* (1913), Hornaday wrote, "When game was plentiful, I believed that it was right for men and boys to kill a limited amount of it for sport and for the table, but times have changed, and we must change also. . . . It is time for the people who don't shoot to call a halt on those who do, and if this be treason, let my enemies make the most of it."[20]

George Bird Grinnell (1849–1938) was a naturalist and one of the United States' earliest anthropologists. He wrote many volumes devoted to the ethnographies of various Plains Indian tribes and became the science editor for one of the earliest periodicals devoted to the growing sport hunting readership, *Forest and Stream* (1873). Grinnell, like Hornaday, was as outspoken in opposition to market hunting as he was in advocating for the conservation of forests and wildlife, though unlike Hornaday, so far as we can tell, he never denounced sport hunting.

Although the conservation movement was preponderantly male, it is important to note that there were a number of women who contributed to the conservation movement. Some, like Martha Maxwell, were avid hunters. A graduate of Oberlin College, she started hunting when she and her husband moved to Colorado. Herman briefly describes her colorful career:

> Maxwell moved to Colorado with her husband in 1860, where she developed her skills as a naturalist, hunter, and taxidermist. The climax of her career came in 1876, when she exhibited a prize-winning diorama of mounted game animals—specimens she had shot (and had herself mounted)—at the Colorado-Kansas entry of the Centennial Exhibition in Philadelphia. Above buffalo, elk, and mule deer,

Maxwell—an ardent advocate of women's rights—
placed a sign that read "Women's Work."[21]

Women, some hunters and some not, also played a leading role in such emergent environmental debates as the
campaign to ban the killing of birds for their plumage,
then used to decorate fashionable women's hats and apparel, and the movement to cease commercial logging in
the redwood forests of the Pacific Northwest.

There are two traditions of Euro-American hunting in
North America. On the one hand, from the earliest colonial
times through the period of westward expansion, hunting
was an essential part of the pioneer way of life; it was a
matter of survival. On the other, and in conformity with
customs brought over from Europe, hunting was seen as a
leisure pursuit of the "landed gentry"; it was by and large a
form of recreation. Women's hunting figured prominently
from the beginning in the pioneer tradition: homesteading
women had to be as adept with long guns as their menfolk
were as well as able when necessary to fend for and defend
themselves and their families. It has been said, only half
jokingly, that a pioneer woman needed only three things: a
rifle, horse, and man. And the man—well, he was expend-
able. Sharpshooter Annie Oakley (b. Phoebe Ann Mosey,
1860) was the embodiment of this pioneer ideal, becoming
the first bona fide female superstar as "Little Sure Shot"

in Buffalo Bill's Wild West show. While celebrated for her trick shooting, she was equally passionate about hunting.

Oakley had her share of company in the field. Hunting caught fire among US English women of means, and especially in more affluent circles, women were admitted to the "hunting fraternity" in the late nineteenth and early twentieth centuries. This was in part a result of the first wave of US feminism. It was also, and perhaps more especially, because hunting itself was under attack due, as we have seen, to the rise of market hunting along with the resulting extinction of the passenger pigeon and near extinction of the American bison. Proponents of the idea of a fair chase saw that it was to their advantage to popularize the idea of hunting by women. Outdoorswomen were featured in hunting magazines as well as advertisements for hunting gear and guns.

A few examples can, for our purposes, capture the depth and breadth of women's hunting in the late nineteenth and early twentieth centuries. Grace Gallatin Seton Thompson (1872–1959), a US journalist and avid hunter, started out as a debutante in New York society, but wound up falling in love with the noted naturalist Ernest Seton Thompson on a voyage abroad. After their return from a shipboard romance and outdoor adventures that sparked Grace's love of both hunting and the outdoors, the two married. Grace wrote *A Woman Tenderfoot* (1900) and *Nimrod's Wife* (1907)—the first how-to primers on women's hunting—including tips on how to dress and the female's place in camp society. With her husband, she cofounded the Girl Pioneers, later called the Campfire Girls, which was similar to the Girl Scouts.

As a rich young widow and brilliant writer, Agnes Herbert's (1870–1960) adventures with her cousin Cecily in Africa, Asia, and North America were recorded in such works as *Two Dianas in Alaska* and *Two Dianas in Somaliland*. They are believed to have been the first women to travel on safari (with guides native to the area).

Paul (Paulina) Brandreth's (1885–1946) *Trails of Enchantment* (1930) is to this day widely regarded as the best book ever written about northeastern whitetail deer hunting in the Adirondacks. Paulina would today be recognized as transgender.

Courtney Borden (1899–1995) was the first woman to participate in an Arctic walrus hunt, which she wrote about in *The Cruise of the Northern Light* (1927), and subsequently in *Adventures in a Man's World: The Initiation of a Sportsman's Wife* (1933). Interestingly, though clearly aligning herself with the emergent sport hunting ethos, she also chronicled the importance of pot hunting for southern communities suffering from poverty during the Great Depression—an expression of the early feminist concern for not only gender inequality but race and class inequality too.

Mary Hastings Bradley (1882–1976) and her husband, Herbert, accompanied taxidermist and naturalist Carl Akeley on successive trips to Africa, including the hunt that produced the "big male of Karasimbi" for the African Gallery of the Natural History Museum in New York City. It must be borne in mind that before the rise of cinema and the travel possibilities it suggested to a growing tourist class, such taxidermic displays—dating back to those of Maxwell—were a popular way of educating the public about environmental facts and fallacies.

As historian Tara Kathleen Kelly demonstrates, the women who joined men afield wrote about hunting, and had in common an impulse toward education as well as a critique of domesticity and the role that women's hunting could play in wildlife awareness. Kelly quotes Seton to make this point emphatically: "Dear woman who goes hunting with her husband, be sure that you have it understood that you do no cooking, or dish washing. . . . You are taking a vacation."[22]

This at least partial rejection of domesticity changed in the post–World War II midcentury, when as we have seen with regard to the hunting hypothesis, patriarchal gender roles became the social standard. Women were urged to leave the labor force, and hunting was defined as a male prerogative. Middle- and most upper-class women were at this point effectively banned from the hunting camp, although some of their rural and working-class counterparts continued the hunting tradition of their pioneer forebears. As we will see in the next chapter, this return to female domesticity was short-lived.

To make a long and inspiring story short, the last third of the nineteenth century and first two decades of the twentieth century saw a dramatic shift in how people understood and came to regard natural resources in the United States, including, of course, wildlife, but also unusual geological formations (think of the Grand Canyon), forests, and rivers and lakes. Yellowstone National Park was created in 1872, and Yosemite in 1890. Teddy Roosevelt added six new national parks totaling 125 million square miles during his nearly eight years (September 1901 to March 1909) as president. He also declared the Grand Canyon a national monument in 1908. In addition, he created the US Forest Service (1905) and appointed Gifford Pinchot its first director to manage the vast stretches of the nation's publicly owned forests. Pinchot, like Roosevelt, was an avid sport hunter and opponent of market hunting. In 1906, Roosevelt dedicated Wyoming's Devils Tower as the first national monument—and significant recognition of Native American religion and rights.

Well before the creation of the Forest Service, the US Commission of Fish and Fisheries was established in 1871 with the charge of protecting as well as restoring the nation's fishery. In 1886, the Bureau of Biological Survey was created with the charge of monitoring the nation's fauna. (The two agencies were combined in 1940, creating the US Fish and Wildlife Service.)

At the same time as the reach of the federal and state governments into resource management was expanding, private citizens, many of them wealthy, were banding together to purchase land for their hunting and fishing pleasure, hiring locals to keep trespassers out. In effect, they were replicating the aristocratic practices of England and the Continent. The Adirondacks in northern New York boasted a number of these elite hunting and fishing retreats, and other retreats were established throughout the country over the course of the late nineteenth and early twentieth centuries. In the decade 1870–1880, the number of these clubs increased rapidly, from thirty-four 4to over three hundred. Some were named after the town or county within which they were located, but others were named after figures like Audubon and Forester (Herbert), who as we've seen, had an enormous impact on establishing the identity of the sportsman/woman who combined a love of the hunt, respect for their quarry, and naturalist's sensibility.[23]

The half century from 1870 to 1920 marked an inflection point that few observers have noted. By the 1870s, the US economy had generated considerable wealth, which then, as now, flowed upward. Though the economy went through severe downturns (half the years of the 1870s–1890s were ones of depression), the era was called the Gilded Age for good reason. There were plenty of wealthy people who faced a stark choice, as described by Herman:

> To save hunting as a rite of Americanness, however, [sport] hunters had to save game, and to save game they had to rely on government. The alternative was either the extirpation of game or the privatization of hunting, neither of which were palatable to most Americans. Consequently, the individualism so cherished by hunters gave way to organization as hunters formed clubs and lobbied government.[24]

Spurred by the likes of Hornaday, Grinnell, Roosevelt, Pinchot, and dozens and dozens of lesser-known writers who wrote for the rapidly growing "hook-and-bullet" readership, the network of hunting organizations expanded beyond clubs that offered members private access to hunting and fishing to include organizations that were explicitly devoted to influencing legislation. The most notable among these groups was the Boone and Crockett Club, founded in 1887 by Roosevelt. The initial one hundred members was a veritable who's who of the United States' elite. Charter members included Hornaday, Grinnell, Pinchot, Senator Henry Cabot Lodge, several lawmakers, and Owen Wister, the author of the 1902 widely read novel *The Virginian*.

It's hard to overestimate the influence that Boone and Crockett wielded. In addition to urging expansion of the national parks and national forests, the club was instrumental in lobbying for legislation that for all practical purposes, ended market hunting. Club member and congressman John F. Lacey introduced a bill, the Lacey Game and Wild Birds Preservation and Disposition Act, passed in 1900, that made the interstate traffic in illegally killed wildlife illegal. By 1900, many states, at the urging of Boone and Crockett along with like-minded organizations that had arisen in the 1870s and 1880s, had established laws aimed at regulating the taking of game. The states instituted seasons that prohibited hunting during those times of the year (for instance, mating seasons) when game was most vulnerable. They also prohibited the taking of females for those species where males and females could readily be distinguished. (Male deer, for example, can impregnate multiple does so the population of bucks can be reduced without jeopardizing the number of fawns produced each year.) In addition, states began setting "bag limits," which are the number of deer, ducks, or other game animals that can legally be taken daily and seasonally. The net effect of these state regulations and the

Lacey act meant that market hunting was effectively made illegal. That, of course, depended on the states' and federal government's ability to enforce the laws. As we noted earlier, many game laws had been on the books for years, some dating to the 1700s, but they were rarely enforced. Nevertheless, again at the prodding of organizations like the Boone and Crockett Club, states started to hire game wardens to enforce the regulations.

The hunters who rallied around the model of the sport hunter promoted by Forester, Grinnell, and the Boone and Crockett Club were advancing a classic example of enlightened self-interest. To withdraw to their private retreats would have risked broad public censure in what was fundamentally a democratic culture, albeit raw and filled with contradictions. Even in the southern states, where owners of large plantations affected the style of the English landed elite and formed exclusive fraternal hunting clubs, they accepted the notion that wild game, as the Georgia court had ruled early on, could not be regarded as private property. Had the elite retreated to their private hunting estates and let the rest hunt without restraint, it would have left an impoverished, ravaged countryside of the sort Marsh had warned. While they took care that they would have private reserves where they could hunt and fish without having to rub elbows with the hoi polloi, they elected to use their considerable influence to promote regulations that would preserve not only game but also broad public access to areas suitable for hunting, with the proviso that hunting would be regulated and the regulations would be enforced. But there were contradictions in this commitment to public access.

Among the contradictions embedded in this extremely important inflection point was a disdain for the market and pot hunters. Market hunters were, virtually by definition, the unwashed lower class. Pot hunters included the rural poor, former slaves in the South, and recent immigrants trapped in low-wage factory jobs. They hunted for food, but hunting was also a respite from dreary jobs, and crucial to their role as male breadwinners and sense of self-sufficiency.[25]

Not surprisingly, the hunters who had enjoyed unfettered access to game did not take kindly to restrictions on what they regarded as a right. The rural Yankees in the Adirondacks objected to the private hunting reserves, and the illegality of hunting a deer no doubt added an extra bit of excitement to the hunt. The conflicts never gave rise to local versions of Robin Hood's exploits, but there were occasional violent confrontations between gamekeepers and local trespassers.[26] Conflicts became more frequent with the shift from private gamekeepers begun in the early twentieth century. The gamekeepers were typically recruited from the local population; the game wardens who replaced them were backed by state law and had more tenuous roots in the communities they policed.

As historian Louis Warren emphasizes, the targets of the game wardens were often recent immigrants for whom they had little sympathy.

Warren uses the 1906 murder of a warden, L. Seely Houk, charged with enforcing the game laws in western Pennsylvania, to illuminate this more general problem.[27] The flood of immigrants that arrived in the late nineteenth century, largely from southern and eastern Europe, were generally looked down on by those who had emigrated to the United States earlier and from Great Britain and northern Europe. Houk's sights were fixed on the immigrant Italian laborers who showed little respect for the game laws and even less respect for Houk. Warren makes it clear that the Italian workers killed the warden.

Another historian, Scott Giltner, describes how southern white elites, who were willing to enlist slaves and, after Emancipation, free Blacks in their sporting pursuits, used the conservation ethos to criminalize independent Black hunters for whom hunting was an important source of subsistence. It's worth quoting Giltner:

> The sporting field became, for blacks, a place of economic opportunity where valuable wildlife, marketing opportunities, and steady employment awaited them. . . . Yet they also helped elite whites reconstruct a racial hierarchy swept away by Emancipation. For Southern elites, particularly

landowners, the sporting field became both a site where they celebrated continued mastery over people of color by re-creating the old master-servant relationship and an arena in which they expressed their fears about black liberation through their antipathy toward unrestricted customary rights. For sportsmen, in Southern hunting and fishing they celebrated their own traditions and acumen and, at the same time, lamented blacks' apparent rejection of whites' sporting codes, a rejection that both threatened fish and game supplies and challenged whites' sporting dominion.[28]

As states worked to enforce the new game laws, exposing wardens to danger, the federal government also faced similar challenges on federal lands, especially the national parks. In addition to his account of the resistance to game laws in the Adirondacks, Jacoby documents how settlers, most of whom were not recent immigrants from eastern or southern Europe, routinely illegally grazed their livestock in and took game from Yellowstone. Ultimately, the US Army had to be enlisted to bring law and order to the park.

With the benefit of hindsight, it is probably the case that without the example of wealthy white elites, both men and women, the stereotypical image of the sport hunter would never have developed, though Jacoby suggests that the pot hunters did have their own version of limiting the harvest of game. Still, it must be said that many of the proponents of the new sporting ethic and new laws governing the taking of game held views of market and pot hunters that were chauvinistic, and in some cases, flat-out racist. Madison Grant was a prominent example of this. Grant was a founding member of the Boone and Crockett Club as well as a major force in the conservation movement. He cofounded the Save the Redwood League (1918), Bronx Zoo, and American Bison Society, and was an advocate for Glacier National Park, among many other conservation causes. But he was also a leading eugenicist, founder of the Eugenics Society and Immigration Restriction League, and author of a blatant racialist tract, "The Passing of the Great Race" (1916), a plea to keep "inferior races" from emigrating to the United States. He was not alone; the Sierra Club, in response to the 2020 summer of Black Lives Matter soul-searching, acknowledged that its legendary founder, John Muir, held views similar to those of Grant. Roosevelt also endorsed misanthropic views of recent immigrants and former slaves.

It took roughly a generation or so to win over the general ranks of the nation's hunters to accept the sportsman ideal. The steady work of the hook-and-bullet press in promoting the ideal and work of elite clubs like the Boone and Crockett began to convince most hunters to accept the new game laws along with the ethic of the fair chase that was the essence of the sporting ideal. Boone and Crockett first codified "fair chase" in 1888 as the fifth article in the new club's bylaws, and it became a sort of catechism of sport hunting. The original statement reads,

> Fair Chase, as defined by the Boone and Crockett Club, in the ethical, sportsmanlike, and lawful pursuit and taking of any free-ranging wild, native North American big game animal in a manner that does not give the hunter an improper advantage over such animals.
>
> Hunter Ethics. Fundamental to all hunting is the concept of conservation of natural resources. Hunting in today's world involves the regulated harvest of individual animals in a manner that conserves, protects, and perpetuates the hunted population. The hunter engages in a one-on-one relationship with the quarry and his or her hunting should be guided by a hierarchy of ethics related to hunting, which includes the following tenets:
>
> 1. Obey all applicable laws and regulations.
>
> 2. Respect the customs of the locale where the hunting occurs.
>
> 3. Exercise a personal code of behavior that reflects favorably on your abilities and sensibilities as a hunter.

4. Attain and maintain the skills necessary to make the kill as certain and quick as possible.

5. Behave in a way that will bring no dishonor to either the hunter, the hunted, or the environment.

6. Recognize that these tenets are intended to enhance the hunter's experience of the relationship between predator and prey, which is one of the most fundamental relationships of humans and their environment.[29]

It is fair to say that framing the hunt as an ethical relationship to both wildlife and, more broadly, nature itself started to give hunting *and hunters* a newfound legitimacy. Not only that, it broadened support for conservation that went well beyond the ranks of hunters, who after all, were a minority of the population.

This increased support was both rhetorical and concrete. States and the federal government began to allocate money to support the recovery of habitat and game populations. Licenses to hunt purchased for a small fee flowed into the coffers of state agencies set up to promote hunting (and fishing). Land grant universities initiated programs to encourage the application of science to the management of game so that seasons for legal hunting could be carefully crafted to maximize reproduction and bag limits could be adjusted to maintain robust populations.

It took several decades for the benefits of these converging developments to become apparent, and several unrelated factors helped to accelerate the recovery of game in the first decades of the twentieth century. World War I drew many hunting-aged men into combat, reducing hunting pressure on wildlife. The depression that befell the agricultural economy after the war led to a recovery of wildlife habitat as fields and pastures lay fallow with the foreclosure of farms. The stock market crash in 1929 that ushered in the Great Depression no doubt produced an uptick in pot hunting, which ironically was a reasonable response to unemployment because game had started to recover. Though the motive was food on the table and not necessarily the playing out of the sportsman's ideal, the laws and applied science that allowed game to recover were vindicated; even the most dedicated pot hunter could see the results of the new rules. Enlightened self-interest began to percolate from the upper to the middle to the working classes.

This change in orientation is hard to measure directly before the era of public opinion polling, which we will examine later, but there were several important pieces of legislation enacted during the Depression years, significant not only for wildlife and hunting, but because even in those severely lean years, hunters supported the legislation even though it raised the cost of hunting. The first was the Migratory Bird Hunting and Conservation Stamp Act, passed in 1934. The act created what quickly became known as the "duck stamp," required of all waterfowl hunters. The funds went directly to support the expansion of what had been a poorly funded patchwork of refuges. In effect, hunters were taxing themselves in order to enhance habitat for migratory birds (including nongame species). To date, the duck stamp has raised well over $100 million and has allowed the purchase of over six million acres of habitat.

The second piece of legislation, the Federal Aid in Wildlife Restoration Act (1937), also known as the Pittman-Robertson Act, named for its two sponsors, directed that an excise tax on the sale of guns and ammunition that had gone into general revenues be dedicated to funding state fish and game agencies. The tax has since been expanded to include archery equipment. A companion act, the Magnuson-Stevens Act, taxing fishing gear, was enacted in 1976. The tax is collected by the US Fish and Wildlife Service, and is allocated to the state agencies that are charged with managing fish and game. The money supports habitat work, wildlife management, scientific research aimed at enhancing wildlife, and hunter education programs. To date, over $5 billion have been raised by this tax.

The first of what are fondly called "critter organizations," dedicated to the promotion of a particular species or family of related species, was founded in 1937. Since its inception, Ducks Unlimited has preserved over twelve million acres of waterfowl habitat in the United States and currently (2019) boasts 737,000 members, with chapters in every state. Hunters were being mobilized to support the cause of conservation in order to undo as much as possible the damage that market hunting and unchecked habitat destruction had done, not only to game, but to wildlife and the land in general.

By the end of the Great Depression, the divergence of the hunting cultures of the "Old World" and United States became consolidated. Access to hunting in England and on the Continent remained restricted largely to the elites, and game was managed to provide the elites with ample opportunities for elaborate hunts. The careful management of game was matched—and in some countries, exceeded—by rigorous exams to quality for a hunting license. In Germany, for example, prospective hunters must pass an exam that tests both detailed knowledge of weapons and an equally detailed knowledge of the natural history as well as habitat needs of the entire range of game animals. The material for each section of the test is contained in an over two-hundred-page handbook on which the hunter is tested.

As we have seen, the United States' elites resisted the temptation to emulate the aristocratic model of game management by restricting access to hunting. Perhaps Grinnell, Roosevelt, and their followers feared the probable wrath of a citizenry hostile to aristocratic privilege (the same period that produced the conservation movement was one of labor strife, a mass migration of former slaves from the South to the northern industrial cities, and socialist-inspired critiques of capitalism). Or more generously, perhaps the upper-class men and women who promoted the conservation movement were themselves committed to the public trust doctrine that held that wildlife was a public good—wild animals belonged equally to everyone—and access to hunting should be open to all. Instead of class-based restrictions on access to hunting, it was thought that restrictions should follow science-based rules and regulations, thus ensuring access to all who wanted to hunt. This was a novel model of game and human management, and it was quickly adopted by Canada. It was formally codified in 2001 and called the North American Model of Wildlife Conservation. It rests on seven tenets, each of which was rooted in the conservation movement of the late nineteenth and early twentieth centuries: wildlife is a public trust resource; markets for game are eliminated; the taking of game is regulated by law; wildlife should only be killed for legitimate purposes and fully utilized; wildlife is an international resource; science is the proper tool for setting wildlife policies; and access to hunting should be democratic.[30] The ways in which each of these models, the European and North American ones, have played out will be explored in the remaining chapters.

FROM DEPRESSION
TO AFFLUENCE

Realigning Our Relationship to Nature

A second world war, and one that carried on for a longer stretch than World War I, dramatically reduced the hunting pressure on wildlife. With habitat recovering as a result of the conservation efforts of the previous decades, even five years of low hunting pressure can yield robust population growth. The respite produced an abundance of game that in many regions of the country had not been seen for decades. It is hard to be precise about the recovery of individual wildlife species, but all signs indicated that the decline of game populations had ended, at least for most game species, and the fate of the passenger pigeon, heath hen, and other species had been averted. To be sure, some species, such as sandhill cranes, needed more time to recover and so they remained protected until hunting began being allowed in 2005 when one flyway in the Midwest was cleared for a short hunting season.

Interest in hunting grew in response to the increasing numbers of deer, ducks, and pheasants, three of the most popular game animals. Yet the increasing sales of hunting licenses was driven by more than the increase in game. The soldiers returning from the war found jobs in the factories that had been unionized, and after the austerity of the war years, the unions quickly bargained for higher wages, a forty-hour workweek, and paid vacations. The GI Bill, signed into law in 1944, offered returning veterans a number of benefits, the most important for our purposes being low-interest home loans and stipends for pursuing post–high school education. In 1947, on a Long Island, New York, onion farm, the first postwar suburb, the first of several Levittowns, was born. The builder created model homes designed for young couples—what we would now regard as starter homes—and with low-interest federally guaranteed loans in mind. Fourteen hundred homes were sold in the first three hours of going on the market.

With Europe and Japan struggling to rebuild after the devastation of the war, the US economy grew rapidly. Corporations not only expanded their production workforce but also rapidly increased the ranks of their white-collar workforce, eager to absorb the flood of college graduates enabled by the GI Bill. Plunked down in the midst of former farmland, the new suburbanites had easy access to land that was good habitat for recovering game species. License sales increased.

While hunters became more law-abiding, the behavior of many hunters invited disdain. Deer camps reeked of alcohol and coarse language, though this may have begun to change for the better in recent decades.[1] More telling, perhaps, was what can only be described as an appalling safety record. As the number of hunters increased, the rate of accidents increased too. Many of the accidents resulted from self-inflicted injuries due to the unsafe handling of weapons, but there were also unacceptably high rates of injury and death resulting from a hunter mistaking a human, often a hunting partner, for a deer, or simply shooting at a bird and inadvertently hitting a fellow hunter. In states with a large hunting population, accidents could run into the hundreds every fall. To nonhunters, it may well have seemed that during deer season, more hunters were killed or wounded than deer.

New York was the first state to respond to this unacceptable rate of accidental injuries and fatalities. In 1947, the same year that Levittown sprang into existence, New York introduced the first mandatory hunter education course for new hunters. Hunters who had held a hunting license before 1947 were "grandfathered," so the license seekers were overwhelmingly young boys. The primary emphasis of the course was firearms safety, yet the course

To nonhunters, it may well have seemed that during deer season, more hunters were killed or wounded than deer.

stressed the ideal of sportsmanship, ethic of the fair chase, and importance of obeying game laws as well, all of which would help ensure the continued recovery of game.

It did not take many years for the hunter education program to show results; the frequency of hunting accidents declined. More states followed New York's lead, and Pittman Robertson funds from the tax on guns and ammunition supported the expansion of hunter education programs. By the 1990s, all fifty states required hunter education in order to get a hunting license.

In a review of hunting-related injuries and deaths, attorney Doris Lin reported that according to statistics compiled by the International Hunter Education Association, hunting-related accidents involving firearms have recently averaged around a thousand per year. Most accidents involved self-inflicted wounds. Fatalities have rarely exceeded a hundred in any given year and more typically are around twenty-five. The vast majority of these fatalities have resulted in hunters shooting other hunters accidentally. Lin cites a study conducted by two orthopedic surgeons using data from US hospitals concluding that the "incidence of a firearm injury associated with hunting activities is 9 in one million hunting days." Injuries and deaths associated with hunting but not involving guns in fact exceed gun-related injuries and deaths. Lin also cites a study estimating that six thousand injuries are caused by falls from tree stands.[2] Though it understandably gets much attention, a hunter accidentally killing a nonhunter is fortunately a rare event.

It's worth pausing to reflect on this because several important things happened in addition to the welcome substantial reduction of injuries and deaths. Hunter education changed the way hunting traditions had been passed on from one generation to the next. The dramatic reduction in accidents reflected a change in the culture and practice of hunting. As a result, even though the stereotype of the rude, reckless, botbellied, beer-swilling hunter persists (more on this later), the results of improved hunter behavior reduced public anxieties about hunting.

Hunter education also helped new hunters understand and deal with the inevitable mix of remorse and excitement that accompanies killing an animal. We began our analysis of how our Stone Age ancestors created rituals and myths to ease the anxieties that killing arouses in both the hunter and nonhunter. And we have seen how these anxieties surfaced in myths and shaped the spectacles of the hunt in Greco-Roman empires, Great Britain, and India as well as European nations and their colonies. Hunter education in the United States (and the more elaborate versions of certifying hunters in Europe and Japan) has in effect become the equivalent "ritual" that creates a coherent moral universe in which killing an animal is acceptable. As hunting became rule bound and informed by

Hunter education also
helped new hunters
understand and deal
with the inevitable
mix of remorse and
excitement that
accompanies killing
an animal.

the ethic of the fair chase, hunters, especially newly initiated ones, were prepared to deal with the cascade of conflicting emotions that accompany the kill.

By the 1960s, the first wave of the baby boom generation became old enough to enroll in hunter education programs and so the state programs flourished, filled with young boys eager to accompany their fathers into the field. With license sales robust, and the sale of guns and ammunition on the rise, state fish and game agencies had budgets that allowed them to expand efforts to improve habitat for game as well as release pen-raised pheasants and quail in states where these popular game birds could not naturally reproduce in sufficient numbers to provide attractive hunting prospects.

To add support to the work of promoting species recovery, a number of organizations promoting specific game animals followed the lead of Ducks Unlimited; the Ruffed Grouse Society was established in 1961, followed by the Wild Turkey Federation (1973), Pheasants Forever (1982), and the Rocky Mountain Elk Foundation (1984), to name only the most prominent. The Pope and Young Club, modeled after the venerable Boone and Crockett Club, was founded in 1961 to promote hunting with bows and arrows.

It was as if the planets had aligned for the reformers who had promoted the sporting ideal: market hunting had ended, game populations were recovering, hunters were largely obeying the law, accidents were dramatically declining, and the recruitment of new hunters was robust. Matching this success story was another one: the economic reforms of the New Deal coupled with the huge economic stimulus of the GI Bill meant that people in the United States not only had more money to spend because of rising wages but also had more leisure time (think paid vacations) and compelling reason to be optimistic about the future. Hunting aside, people were going camping, visiting state and national parks, fishing, and bird-watching— all in growing numbers. But the planets did not stay aligned for long, and the consequences, especially for hunting, have been striking.

Rapid economic growth and an equally rapid change in where and how people lived set in motion cultural changes with which people in the United States have wrestled ever since. The rapid growth of the suburbs turned out to have a profound effect on the US family. The move from the city to suburbs meant loosening the ties of shared ethnicity and kin networks as young couples left ethnic neighborhoods. Combined with social security and pension plans, aging parents became less dependent on their adult children, and those adult children were relieved of the need to plan for the care of their aging parents. The suburbs were packed with young families. Soon, subdivisions were built in the Sunbelt for retirees, no children allowed (except as visitors). Intergenerational cultural continuities gave way to the "generation gap."

The break with the past, marked by low wages, long hours of labor, and near-constant worries about making ends meet, was sudden. Set against the immediate backdrop of war and depression, the attraction of rising wages, a forty-hour workweek, paid vacations, and easy credit, particularly for veterans, easily trumped the culture of thrift. People went from a culture that emphasized thrift ("use it, wear it out, make do, or do without") to one of "throw it away, get the 'revolutionary new.'" The era of consumer-driven capitalism was born.

The suburbs unleashed a consumer binge; all of these new houses needed appliances (which landlords provided in the rental apartments in the city, but didn't come standard with homeownership). The absence of public transportation meant that growing families needed two cars: husbands needed a car to get to and from work, and wives needed one to get kids to school and doctor's appointments, and run errands. It wasn't long before music lessons, little league, and other adult-organized activities dominated boys' and girls' and moms' (and to a lesser extent, dads') schedules.

There were also more subtle but no less important consequences of moving to the suburbs. With everything new, including neighbors, new norms needed to be established. It was okay to occasionally call on a neighbor for a favor or cup of flour to save a special trip to the shopping center, but doing so too often would run the risk of being judged a poor homemaker. Similarly, borrowing tools too frequently or failing to return borrowed tools in good working order risked social standing. The US ideal of self-sufficiency that allowed pioneers to endure deprivation was transposed into a requirement to have everything needed to keep the yard manicured and household fully equipped with all the "laborsaving" appliances, not to mention tasteful (whose taste?) furnishings.[3]

After World War II, the return to normal was promoted as if the script was plagiarized from the hunting hypothesis, except now it was no longer merely a hypothesis. The nation's leading psychologists, sociologists, psychiatrists, and physicians were virtually unanimous in extolling the husband as breadwinner and wife as homemaker nuclear family as the arrangement ideally adapted to the modern, industrial, urban/suburban society. Moreover, it's the family arrangement that evolution prepared us for. Women were laid off, and their factory jobs were filled by returning veterans. The small number of women who had hunted became even smaller as working- and middle-class women were urged to embrace domesticity with the same enthusiasm that their husbands were presumably investing in their jobs.

In 1963, feminist activist Betty Friedan published her blockbuster, *The Feminine Mystique*. Friedan peeled away the veneer of domestic bliss, revealing wives frustrated and depressed by domesticity, and unsatisfied with taking vicarious pleasure in the accomplishments of husbands and children. To make matters more fraught, it turned out that consumer spending was increasing faster than most husbands' wages and salaries. The result was rapidly mounting household debt. In addition to mortgage and auto loans, consumers piled on credit card debt. In the years from 1947 to 1969, disposable family income increased fourfold. At the same time, mortgage debt increased elevenfold and short-term consumer credit (such as auto loans and credit card debt) increased by a factor of sixteen.[4]

Wives began returning to the workforce, in a trickle at first, but rapidly accelerating as children became old enough to get along without having mom at home when they returned from school. The immediate effect of dual-earner households was that parents had less time to spend with their kids, and the time they did spend was often shuttling kids to practices, games, and music lessons. Finding time for a youngster to squeeze in a hunter education course in a crowded calendar was a challenge, even for youngsters who were interested in hunting with dad.

Meanwhile, women's desire for fuller participation in the world outside the home revealed tensions in relationships that had been impossible to acknowledge.[5] Friedan called this "the problem that has no name."[6] In effect, husbands and wives drifted apart, each consumed by the demands of their respective spheres. The divorce rate began to rise. Once largely confined to the poor and the world of celebrity, divorce suddenly hit the middle class.[7] This quickly started to have an impact on the recruitment of young boys to hunting. Divorce weakened the traditional father-son path of recruitment to hunting. The allure of team sports and conveniently timed invention of video games competed with the attraction of hunting with dad, especially when dad was only available for a few days a month, if that.

The rapid growth in the economy, boosted by the rapid growth of the suburbs, and the ways both reshaped and weakened the family, was accompanied by equally dramatic shifts in US culture that also had an impact on hunting, both directly and indirectly. Sparked by conservationist Rachel Carson's book *Silent Spring* (1962), a new environmental consciousness emerged. Building on yet going well beyond the traditional conservation movement of Teddy Roosevelt, Gifford Pinchot, and their allies, this new "environmentalism" was critical of the multiple ways in which the government agencies created by the conservationists had become captives of the industries they were intended to oversee. Some industries, notably the chemical giants like DuPont, were scarcely regulated at all, and the research that was spurred by the two world wars had led to hundreds of largely untested chemicals being introduced each year in the form of pesticides, herbicides, and industrial compounds that found their way into the burgeoning consumer markets (think plastics, PCBs, and nonstick cookware).

Eight years after *Silent Spring*, the first Earth Day was celebrated.[8] Hundreds of thousands of people marked the day, and subsequent Earth Days have mobilized millions across the globe. In the planning for the April 22, 1970, Earth Day, as described in detail by historian Adam Rome, only one organization that had a relationship to hunters, the National Wildlife Federation, was peripherally involved. Hunters were simply not thought of as a supportive constituency. It's not clear if any of the organizations that hunters had supported (Boone and Crockett, Ducks Unlimited, and so on) either endorsed or otherwise urged engagement with the original Earth Day or any of the subsequent annual Earth Day observances.

The overwhelming success of Earth Day marked a dramatic shift in how people thought about the environment. The people drawn to the new movement brought disparate and even conflicting agendas, but there was broad agreement on the need to replace or at least balance the anthropocentric perspective of the conservation movement with a more biocentric view. Ironically, a hunter's posthumously published book of essays, *A Sand County Almanac* (1947), was rediscovered and became one of the inspirations for

The overwhelming success of Earth Day marked a dramatic shift in how people thought about the environment.

the new environmental movement. The author, Aldo Leopold, was a leading conservationist, founder of the Wilderness Society, and pioneering figure in the new science of game management. Yet what drew a new audience to Leopold was not his love of hunting or even the scientific management of game that he promoted; it was his advocacy of what he called "the land ethic." Leopold condemned the human impulse to control nature, or in his words, to be "conquerors" of the land, and urged us to become "plain citizens" of the biotic community, taking care, again in his words, "to save every cog and wheel" of the diverse and complex biotic community on which we depended, and of which we were, unavoidably, a member.[9] The idea of plain citizens, with its echo of writer Henry David Thoreau's urging us to simplify, resonated with the celebration of organic farming, woodstoves, solar panels, and critiques of industrial-scale farming, nonrenewable fuels, and nuclear power. But hunting? Not so much.

The new environmental movement grew quickly and led to a rapid increase in environmental advocacy groups. Among the most prominent were Greenpeace (1971), the National Resource Defense Fund (1970), EarthJustice (1971), which grew out of the Sierra Club's Legal Defense Fund, and the Center for Biological Diversity (1989). These high-profile, national organizations, however, were just the tip of an iceberg of local and statewide organizations that began lobbying local and state governments as well as filing lawsuits to protect the environment from public and private projects deemed injurious. There can be little doubt that this upwelling of public concern led to the passage in 1972 of a tightening of the Clean Air Act (1963), Clean Water Act (1972), and Endangered Species Act (1973).

Unlike the earlier conservation movement, hunting organizations were not notably involved in this flurry of activism. But the activism did draw out and energize critiques of hunting and hunters that had been confined to the margins of public concern through the post World War II decades. Though tenuously related to the main concerns of the new environmental advocacy groups (with the exception of Greenpeace's campaign against seal hunts in Canada), the critique of hunting appeared to be a tenet of the environmental movement. Hunters and environmentalists parted ways. Hunters understandably grew defensive, insisting that their support of conservation had kept the country from what would have been an environmental catastrophe. Moreover, hunters proudly claimed that their dollars (through license fees, taxes on guns and ammunition, and the duck stamp) exceeded by orders of magnitude other sources of environmental funding.

The critics pressed their case. There were three basic criticisms. One focused on the alleged ecological damage that hunting entailed. The second critique, promoted by the animal rights movement, argued that because animals are sentient, they deserve to be included in an expanded circle of moral consideration. Both of these objections drew support from a selective reading of Leopold. The third critique revolved around the character of hunters—an objection that as we have seen, has been a constant theme for millennia, depicting hunters as violent, reckless, and more likely to be abusive of pets, children, and spouses—in short, bad actors. Let's look at each briefly here to make the point that the heightened concern for the environment and a renewal of criticism of hunting, combined with the changes we've examined in the family, started to depress interest in hunting.

The ecological critique is straightforward: the dollars spent on conservation have largely gone to enhancing populations of game animals at the expense of other species. To take but one example, white-tailed deer populations have exploded in many areas of the country, and they have had a dramatic and negative effect on the herbivory in many parks as well as city and suburban forests.[10] Indeed, a number of game species have begun to push the limits of ecological carrying capacity. Though the reasons for this are more complicated than some of the critics claim, there can be no doubt that nearly a century of promoting game species has had ecological consequences that were not anticipated. Surging populations of some game species have become a serious management problem, not least by draining resources from what otherwise could be more balanced programs of environmental management that would enhance the overall biodiversity.

In order to boost game populations (and relatedly, protect domestic animals and crops from damage), federal and state governments have long promoted programs to control and even eradicate "bad" animals—most notoriously, the effort to rid the nation of wolves. In the colonial era, colonies offered bounties on wolves, and all manner of poisons, traps, snares, and guns were used to eradicate them. The last wolf in Connecticut was said to have been killed in 1749. Historian Jon Coleman describes in heartrending terms the war waged on wolves.[11] Not content with enlisting bounty hunters in the gory business, the federal government in 1885 established the program called Animal Damage Control, housed in the Branch of Economic Ornithology, which went through several name changes over the years, finally becoming the Wildlife Services, housed in the US Department of Agriculture in 1985. Its mission, however, didn't change: it killed "varmints" that posed a risk to game animals as well as domestic flocks and crops. Journalist Christopher Ketcham writes that "since 2000, Wildlife Services operatives have killed at least 2 million native mammals and 15 million native birds. . . . In 2014, Wildlife Services killed 322 wolves, 61,702 coyotes, 2,930 foxes, 580 black bears, 796 bobcats, five golden eagles and three bald eagles."[12]

Leopold entered the infant US Forest Service in 1909, and was sent to the Southwest to manage the range and national forests there. Among his duties, he was to kill wolves in order to boost the deer population. In one of the most widely quoted passages in *A Sand County Almanac*, he writes about firing on a wolf and her young:

> We reached the old she wolf in time to watch a fierce green fire dying in her eyes. I realized then, and have known ever since, that there was something new to me in those eyes—something known only to her and the mountain. I was young then, and full of trigger itch; I thought that because fewer wolves meant more deer, that no wolves would mean hunters' paradise. But after seeing the green fire die, I sensed that neither the wolf nor the mountain agreed with such a view.[13]

His suspicion was correct. The campaign to remove wolves, coyotes, and mountain lions resulted in the short run in more deer. Deer commenced to overbrowse the habitat, ruining it not only for themselves but also for cattle and the native flora and fauna. In effect, removing the top predator created what we now call a "trophic cascade," negatively affecting entire ecosystems. In the seventy years since Leopold penned those words, we still struggle with the legacy of short-term thinking.

In recent decades, state and federal agencies have started to take a longer view, if not yet "thinking like a mountain," but they are tethered to the income stream that comes from hunters. As author Ron Baker and others have made clear, this has skewed conservation. It has made the claim that hunters are the "true conservationists," even if their claim to be the major source of conservation dollars remains true, seem hollow. This critique, not surprisingly, has been met with hostility by hunters, widening the rift between them and the new environmentalists. Suffice it to say, this critique of hunting along with the resultant split between hunters and environmentalists contributed to reducing the public's acceptance of hunting, and some unmeasurable degree, reduced interest in hunting, especially for those of high school and college age who were galvanized by the new environmental movement.

The animal rights critique of hunting focuses less on the ecological—in fact, it often ignores ecology entirely—than on respecting the lives of individual animals. The movement has its own internal debates and factions to which we cannot do justice here. Despite philosophical differences between the movement's two main theorists, Peter Singer and Thomas Regan, all advocates for animal rights agree that because animals are sentient—they can feel pain and experience emotions much as humans do—they deserve to be left alone to live out their lives on their own terms.[14] There certainly is evidence that animals feel pain, and some species clearly experience emotions, but it is not clear that this should mean that animals should not be killed by humans since they are obviously killed by other animals.[15] It may mean that they should not be killed indiscriminately or gratuitously, yet as we have seen, humans have recognized this (regal excesses excepted) and established various versions of ethical regard for the animals they hunted. Some animal rights advocates acknowledge that it may be acceptable to kill an animal in self-defense or the face of no alternative but starvation (Singer), although others (Regan) won't even concede this. To be sure, these are now extremely rare circumstances, though as we will see in the next chapter, human fatalities from encounters with lions and elephants (Africa) as well as tigers (India and Bangladesh) occur annually.

Since it is now possible to have a healthy diet that avoids meat (vegetarianism) or all animal products (vegan), and use cotton and synthetic fabrics to clothe ourselves, there is no need for wool, furs, or hides for our apparel and accessories. The major organizations promoting animal rights are the Humane Society of the United States and People for the Ethical Treatment of Animals (PETA). The Animal Liberation Front, loosely affiliated with PETA, has carried out direct actions that break the law. These actions have ranged from destroying labs that use animals for experiments to releasing animals from captivity and harassing scientists who engage in research on animals.[16] Although most attention has been directed at the treatment of farm animals and use of animals in scientific research, animal activists have also disrupted hunters, following them into the woods, making noises intended to frighten animals away from the hunters, and protesting live pigeon shoots. In response, several states have passed laws making it a crime to intentionally interfere with hunters.

Protests against hunting have succeeded in ending fox hunting in Britain, and some states in the United States have ended the hunting of mountain lions. A few other states have outlawed some forms of hunting (using dogs to hunt bears, for example), but the animal rights movement has had a larger impact, as we will see later, in some African nations. The animal rights movement has moved the public's attitudes toward more sympathy for wildlife. While the reasons are more complicated than just the work of animal activists, it is clear that the public is more sympathetic to wild animals and more suspect of wildlife managers than was the case when the United States was a largely rural society. Again, it is hard to measure with any degree of precision, but it is likely that sympathy for animals has had a dampening effect on the recruitment of youngsters to hunting.

The third line of criticism has centered on hunters themselves. The fact that most hunters are male has shaped this critique, which in the hands of ecofeminists becomes a charge that males are responsible not only for the violence of hunting but for violence against nature in general too. Writer Joy Williams is a case in point. Confusing the notion of sportsmanship with the trivial, she writes, "For hunters, hunting is fun. Recreation is play. Hunting is recreation. Hunters kill for play, for entertainment. They kill for the thrill of it, to make an animal 'theirs.'" She goes on to assert that "hunters are piggy . . . insatiable, malevolent and vain. They maim and mutilate and despoil."[17] Ecofeminist Marti Kheel goes a step further in characterizing hunters (and by implication, all men): "It is necessary to recognize that the perpetrators of violence throughout the world are, by and large, men, and the victims of this violence are primarily women and the natural world."[18] Even a more measured critic of hunting, anthropologist Matt Cartmill, can't keep from suggesting that hunters are attracted to hunting because it is transgressive:

> In fact . . . wrongness may itself be part of the
> attraction of hunting. Some men . . . seem to enjoy
> feeling evil, and some hunters—say, those who kill
> wild animals for no discernable reason . . . may enjoy
> their sport precisely because it makes them feel wild
> and wicked and crazy . . . [It is] the rural equivalent
> of running through Central Park at night, raping and
> murdering random New Yorkers.[19]

There are no doubt some hunters who are "bad actors." But there is no convincing evidence that demonstrates a correlation between hunting and rape. As for hunters being "insatiable, malevolent and vain," Williams could more legitimately be describing some members of Congress than the twelve million hunters in the United States. There are, unfortunately, too few studies of hunters, but those few studies show that while as a group, hunters are somewhat more politically conservative than the general population, they are in general indistinguishable from their nonhunting neighbors.[20] There is too much violence, and in particular, too much violence toward and abuse of women, yet there is no evidence that hunters are more likely to contribute to this lamentable fact than non- and even antihunters.

There is one additional strand that emerged from the cultural ferment of the 1960s and 1970s that has contributed to a decline in the number of hunters. The rapid growth of suburbs, from the 1950s onward, fueled in part by "white flight," saw increasing Black and impoverished populations in major cities. Blacks had moved north and to the West Coast seeking jobs in factories hungry for workers to meet the demands of the war effort. Having fought a war to defeat an explicitly racist regime, overt segregation at home became increasingly unacceptable. The 1954 Supreme Court decision declaring school segregation unconstitutional triggered the civil rights movement that challenged the Jim Crow laws of the South along with the pattern of discrimination in employment, housing, and education in the North and West. Riots erupted in the 1960s, first in Watts in Southern California, and a year later in Detroit and Newark, New Jersey. Together with the riots, the assassinations of President John F. Kennedy, and then civil rights leader Martin Luther King Jr., and months later, politician Robert Kennedy put the nation on edge. Conservatives called for law and order, and liberals demanded measures to limit access to guns. Neither got what they sought. Protests continued, against an unpopular war as well as racial discrimination. And the sales of guns surged, as they have ever since, after the election of a Democratic president and a succession of mass shootings. But interestingly, the percentage of households owning a gun has steadily decreased over the past three decades. According to the National Opinion Research Center's annual General Social Survey, in 1977, 53.9 percent of US households had at least one firearm, a high point. By 2018, the last date available at this writing, 35.2 percent reported owning a gun.[21] With fewer households possessing a gun, it seems likely that the number of parents encouraging their child's interest in hunting was necessarily declining, especially if neither parent had ever hunted. Unfortunately, there are no hard data that allow us to directly test this bit of conjecture, but there are hard data that bear on this. Every five years, beginning in 1955, the US Fish and Wildlife Service conducts the National Survey of Fishing, Hunting, and Wildlife-Associated Recreation. In 1955, 10 percent of the adult population sixteen years old or older reported having hunted. Scarcely any women hunted then so this meant that roughly 20 percent of the male population hunted. This participation rate stayed steady through the 1960s and 1970s, but it began to decline after 1980. In 1985, 8.4 percent reported having hunted. The decline grew steeper; in 2001, it was 6 percent, and by the latest survey in 2016, the participation rate hit 4 percent. The decline was steepest on the East and West Coasts: 2 percent in California, Oregon, Washington, and New England. Participation was highest in the middle of the country, ranging from a low of 5 percent in the mountain states to a high of 8 percent in the midwestern states.[22]

Hunters are overwhelmingly white. As we've seen, Blacks did hunt in the antebellum South, and as anthropologist Stuart Marks has shown, Blacks still hunt in the rural South, though in numbers fewer than whites.[23] Scott Giltner, mentioned earlier, adds that recent surveys indicate that three-quarters of all Black hunters are in the South.[24] Both Marks and Giltner suggest that the low participation of Blacks can be partially explained by the history of restricting opportunities of the enslaved and, later, freedmen to hunt. Paradoxically, given the passage and enforcement of game laws in the late nineteenth and

early twentieth centuries, along with the rise of the sporting ethic of the fair chase, enslaved peoples were freer to
hunt as they liked than were the freedmen. Though the
game laws were not promulgated solely to constrain Black
hunters, that certainly was the effect in the South.

Beyond that, and more to the point of the contemporary moment, it must also be noted that in both the South
and North today, the Black population is largely an urban
one. The data collected by the US Fish and Wildlife Service
every five years has from the beginning shown that urban
dwellers are less likely than residents of small towns and
rural areas to be hunters. In the latest survey, conducted
in 2016, only 2 percent of the nation's hunters lived in
large metropolitan areas (including the suburbs associated with large cities). Fifty-three percent lived in small
cities and towns. So there is a geographic effect that likely
impacts Black people's interest and participation in hunting. It is worth noting too that much to the dismay of the
National Park Service, Blacks are much less likely than
whites to visit the national parks. Higher rates of poverty
and, more generally, lower wages for Blacks undoubtedly
contribute to lower participation in hunting and park vis-
its. It is also quite possible that Blacks are understandably
worried about how whites might respond to an armed
Black person. Better safe than sorry. Blacks are not inhib-
ited from fishing, however; they constitute 9 percent of
the nation's fishers.

Hunters are also, not surprisingly, largely male, but female participation began rising in the 1990s. By the 2016 survey, 10 percent of all hunters were female. Two-thirds of today's hunters are adults aged thirty-five to sixty-four years old. A small minority are not high school graduates, and most have at least some college education. A large majority of hunters had incomes putting them well above the poverty line. In short, while overwhelmingly white, male, and residents of small cities and towns, in terms of education and income, hunters are predominantly in the middle class, neither rich nor poor.[25]

It's worth noting, by comparison, that while hunters' numbers are declining, interest in wildlife watching has been steadily increasing. Between the 2011 and 2016 US Fish and Wildlife Service surveys, wildlife watchers increased 20 percent, from 71.8 to 86 million. And while Blacks constitute less than 1 percent of the nation's hunters, 3 percent of the wildlife watchers are Black. (The recent episode of a Black birder being harassed by a white dog walker suggests that even Blacks with binoculars arouse fear when they are "out of place."[26]) The growth of wildlife watching reflects the change in attitudes toward wildlife that we mentioned earlier and will now examine more closely.

LIVING WITH WILDLIFE

We have devoted two chapters exclusively to hunting and social change in the United States. But it is important to recognize that though the US experience is distinctive, other nations have also undergone dramatic changes in the past one hundred years—changes that have had an impact on their hunting traditions and practices that reveal critiques of hunting similar to those that US hunters have faced. We will focus on Great Britain, western Europe, sub-Saharan Africa, and India. The former two represent cultures with which the United States wishes to be compared favorably in many respects, hunting included. The latter are examples of former colonies struggling to define themselves in the contemporary world in which environmental concerns weigh heavily on desires to utilize natural resources, including wildlife, to raise standards of living. With all of our differences in history and culture, we are all confronted with deciding how to live with a heightened regard for wildlife that has made hunting controversial. Again, with differences in emphasis, people across the world are being urged to learn to live with wildlife and manage ourselves rather than managing wildlife, especially when managing wildlife means killing.

Great Britain and Europe (both west and east) experienced the equivalent of the ravaging of wildlife that occurred in the United States in the eighteenth and nineteenth centuries, but several centuries earlier. The aurochs, a large cow-like animal, went extinct in 1627 as a result of over-hunting and disease spread from domesticated cattle. The European bison, like its North American namesake, was reduced to a few remnant populations by the eleventh century and is now being kept in a closely managed herd in the primeval Bialowieza Forest in Poland.[1] The forest, now a protected area, was historically kept as the hunting ground for royalty, and after Germany invaded Poland in 1939, it became the playground for Nazi Party leader Hermann Göring, an avid hunter.

As we saw in chapter 2, royal estates became refugia for select game animals, and the estates were managed to keep both commoners and animals that preyed on game at bay. But by the twentieth century, draconian punishments for poaching the "king's game" disappeared, though in many countries general public access was restricted by onerous licensing, required club memberships, or the explicit permission of the landowner (usually for a fee). England, which as we have seen, promulgated some of the harshest penalties for violating game laws, now does not even require a license for the hunting of birds, yet landowner permission is required, and many landowners require fees and even particular apparel for the highly organized hunts. By contrast, hunting in Italy is now regulated only to the extent that a license is required. Licensed hunters are free to hunt on both public and private lands. Hunting in Germany and France remains highly regulated, and, as noted earlier, Germany requires passing a rigorous examination to become a licensed hunter.

Game management in many countries depends heavily on large estate owners, who manage game for profit, and private hunting associations, which also typically own hunting grounds on which they manage game for the pleasure of their members. Many of these associations (they resemble the fraternal organizations in the United States, but are focused on the promotion of hunting) were founded several centuries ago, and zealously guard their traditions and rituals. In England, the British Association for Shooting and Conservation promotes the interests of hunters, and has a membership of over 150,000. Similar associations from across Europe joined hands to form the European Federation for Hunting and Conservation in 1977.

Although hunting traditions across Europe differ, and differ from those in the United States, European hunters have faced challenges similar to those of US hunters. Claims of interest in conservation have been challenged both by animal rights organizations and those who criticize the narrow focus on game animals rather than on ecology as a whole. Animal rights is arguably more influential, particularly in western Europe and Great Britain, than in the United States. The British Labor Party, for example, championed a ban on fox hunting, reflecting both a class animus (remember writer Oscar Wilde's quip, "The unspeakable in full pursuit of the uneatable"[2]) and animal rights objection to the aristocratic sport. Foxes can still be killed in England, however, if they pose a threat to domestic animals or people.

The ecological critique of hunting has a stronger case in Europe than it does in the United States, in part because most European societies have been managing their wildlife for centuries longer than the United States. Indeed, in England, the aristocracy was managing wildlife before the United States became a nation. The problem from an ecological point of view is that the management strategy was designed to sustain desirable game animals, and reduce and even eliminate the "bad" animals that threatened the "good" ones. The result has been an even more truncated wildlife population than that of the United States. As in the case of the United States, this critique has led

The ecological critique
of hunting has a
stronger case in Europe
than it does in the
United States.

to efforts to restore a presumed ecological balance, variously described as ecological restoration and rewilding. These efforts include restoring ecosystems to their pre-disturbance status, which entails intensive management, but management directed at reproducing more or less the full complement of the original diversity of species. One of the most ambitious of these restorations is an attempt in the Netherlands to create a replica of what the prehuman landscape of Europe looked like. The Oostvaardersplassen is a twenty-three-square-mile reserve a short drive from Amsterdam.[3] The reserve was designed to test the controversial idea of Franz Vera, an ecologist who has made a career of debunking the idea that the prehuman landscape was a primeval forest—a dark, closed canopy of mature forest. Instead, Vera has argued that the combination of large mammals (grazers, browsers, and predators) and smaller mammals, birds, and insects formed a community that created a patchwork of mature forest, savanna, and brushy edges that supported the varied needs, both for food and protection from weather and predators, of a biotically rich and diverse ecosystem.

Vera's experiment promises to be instructive, but unlike the original landscape, which reproduced itself over thousands, if not millions, of years, the Oostvaardersplassen is too small and hemmed in by an intensively humanized landscape to ever be self-replicating. It will require sustained human management at least as intensive as anything the landed aristocracy did and as current professional wildlife managers do. And to make things more vexed, maintaining the menagerie that the Oostvaardersplassen has attracted has required culling. Indeed, in recent years Vera's project has been mired in controversy. There have been large-scale die-offs of some species whose numbers could not be sustained on the reserve. Animal protectionists illegally brought in feed for the starving animals, as pictures of emaciated animals aroused public outrage. Vera was the target of death threats.[4]

Even where large space is available, as it is theoretically in the arid western United States, restoration requires management—and breeds controversy. Two proposals to carry out large-scale restoration projects in the West—one called the Buffalo Commons, proposing to let the prairie states return to the days when the "buffalo roamed," and the other called Pleistocene Rewilding, bringing to the western plains proxies for the megafauna that went extinct some twelve thousand years ago—are Oostvaardersplassen on steroids.[5] But restoration projects are not an answer to those who find management itself repugnant.

George Monbiot, a widely read British journalist who focuses on environmental issues, makes a case for letting nature take its course. Monbiot describes how he arrived at his current position. After getting a degree in ecology and working for the BBC's natural history unit, he traveled abroad to West Papua, then Brazil, and then East Africa, where he saw a much less manicured and domesticated nature than was typical of England. He writes,

> Coming home, it took me a while to notice something odd. Here (in England), many conservationists appear to believe . . . that the diversity, integrity, and "health" of the natural world depend upon human intervention, often intense intervention, which they describe as "management" or "stewardship." More often than not, this involves clearing trees and using cattle and sheep to suppress the vegetation. To a lesser extent, the same belief prevails in several other parts of the rich world. Some of our conservation groups appear to be not just zoophobic, but also dendrophobic: afraid of trees. They seem afraid of the disorderly, unplanned, unstructured revival of the natural world.[6]

Essentially, Monbiot argues that if we simply stop manipulating nature, nature will rewild itself, reviving the cliché that "nature knows best." Monbiot has a point. If we may rely on another cliché, "nature abhors a vacuum": left to itself, natural processes will fill in the vacuum. For generations of ecologists, it was assumed that nature would fill the vacuum in an orderly process called succession, by which, step by step, nature would slowly but surely reproduce the original, predisturbed ensemble of plant and animal species. Monbiot is not opposed to tweaking this process—he applauds the return of wolves to Yellowstone—but he suggests that it is likely that wolves would have made the return on their own were it not for the active hostility toward wolves of the ranchers who in effect formed a barrier to dispersing wolves from Canada. Whether or not this is so, this bit of rewilding has not been nearly the ecological success story that Monbiot and others have claimed. Wolves have indeed had an impact on the park's ecology, but the impact is far less dramatic than Monbiot indicates.[7]

Monbiot cites a number of instances in which rewilding is occurring without much, if any, human encouragement. One example whose return he applauds is the boar. It's useful to focus on this animal because in recent decades, the wild boar and its cousin, the feral pig, have become common across Europe, are increasing in England, and are plentiful in a number of states in the United States. From the standpoint of "natural" rewilding, the boar is as good an illustration as can be found. Monbiot acknowledges that boars damage row crops as well as orchards and vineyards, yet he passes this off by pointing to the positive contributions that boars make to the landscape—their rooting about encourages plant diversity and improves the fertility of the soil—and is at pains to debunk fears that boars pose a threat to humans. This is a bit odd since one of his assertions in favor of spontaneous rewilding is that it makes our staid, orderly, and ultimately boring nature more dynamic, surprising, and challenging. An encounter with a big boar with tusks would certainly not be boring, even if the animal shows no interest in attacking.

But here's the problem. Boars have high rates of fertility, and at present, face virtually no predators capable of constraining their numbers. In northern Italy, the animals—which can weigh up to five hundred pounds—are severely impacting vineyards. Denmark has completed a boar-proof fence along the entire Denmark-German border to keep wild boars from interfering with the lucrative Danish pork industry. This is made all the more urgent because free-ranging boars infected with African swine fever, a highly contagious disease, have begun showing up in several European nations (Belgium and Slovakia as of this writing in 2021). The disease causes high mortality in wild and domestic pigs. Endemic in Africa, it has appeared in China and forced the destruction of tens of thousands of pigs in an effort to contain the disease. So far, wild and domestic pigs in the United States have not been exposed to the disease, in part thanks to a rigorous screening of pork products coming from China.

In fairness, the problems that the resurgent boar population have begun to impose are not apparent in Great Britain or much of Europe, but the odds are in favor of problems. As we've noted, the centuries of managing both for agriculture and game animals has simplified biotic communities across Great Britain and Europe. Though there are small, remnant populations of bears and wolves in scattered refugia, the physical barriers to dispersal are daunting and the social barriers add to the poor prospects for Monbiot's plan in Europe. For example, in 2005, a bear that made its way from Austria, where it is estimated there are thirty bears, to Bavaria caused a considerable stir. The *Guardian* reported that "the euphoria was short-lived, however; Bavaria's environment minister said hunters were free to shoot it. [Politician] Werner Schnappauf described the bear as 'out of control,' and said: 'We can't take the risk that it harms humans.'"[8] Learning to live with resurgent wildlife is, it turns out, easier said than done. This is so with animals that have long been absent from peoples' daily lives, and as we will see next, it is also a challenge to live with wildlife that are a familiar presence in daily life.

One of the reasons that many large wild animals have gone extinct or been reduced to remnants confined in parks and refugia is that they are incompatible with modern industrial societies. Imagine what the autobahn would be like if herds of aurochs were still around in large numbers. Or imagine the Swiss train schedules if trains had to wait for European bison intent on crossing the tracks. In more rural areas, living with wildlife can mean a ruined crop in a night's visit from elephants passing through, or a villager dragged into the bush for a lion's or tiger's dinner. The stakes are much higher in contemporary societies struggling to feed growing populations. The situation in developing countries in sub-Saharan Africa is complex, not least because US and European conservation groups, animal rights groups, and organizations promoting trophy hunting, like the Safari Club International (founded in 1972), each for their own reasons have exerted strong pressure on African nations to protect the last truly wild large mammal populations left on the planet: the elephants, large ungulates and their predators, and our close cousins, the chimps and great apes.

Of course, there is considerable variation from one postcolonial nation to another in terms of hunting and game management. Kenya is at one extreme. In the late 1960s and early 1970s, the population of elephants in Kenya plummeted from over two hundred thousand to less than thirty thousand. The market for ivory attracted local hunters eager to cash in on the lucrative trade. In 1973, Kenya banned the hunting of elephants to the applause of conservation and animal rights groups. This coalition urged Kenya to extend the ban on hunting elephants to a virtual ban on all hunting, which Kenya did in 1977. By contrast, Tanzania encourages hunting, including revenue-generating trophy-hunting safaris and subsistence hunting for citizens. Hunting for the latter is regarded as an inalienable right. Despite the variations, virtually all

African nations confront the same fundamental challenges posed by wildlife: growing human populations. Africa has some of the most rapidly growing populations in the world, which inevitably means human encroachments on wildlife habitat and the equally inevitable conflict between humans and wildlife are increasing. The need to feed a growing population and raise its standard of living has led to sharp divisions.[9]

One development strategy is to use robust wildlife populations to attract ecotourism. This is the path taken by Kenya and some other nations; Botswana and Zambia have recently banned trophy hunting; and others are contemplating banning the hunting of specific animals. The ban on hunting is intended to create large populations of wildlife that will draw ecotourists from Europe and North America. The problems with this strategy, explored in great detail by journalists Glen Martin and Mark Dowie, are manifold.[10] Protecting wildlife from locals who are intent on protecting their livestock and crops is difficult. For instance, the Maasai, who measure their wealth in terms of cattle, have a long tradition in which young men earn their place in adult society by tracking and killing lions that have attacked their cattle. Outlawing the killing of lions has made this traditional rite of passage a criminal act. Ironically, in Tanzania, where hunting is legal, a small nonprofit, African People and Wildlife, has recruited fifty young Maasai men to be "lion monitors," using their skills in tracking lions to assist shepherds in preventing lion predation. In effect, these young men are protecting both cattle and lions, confirming their hunting skills while sparing the lion. As one of the monitors observed, "It will be shameful if we kill them [lions] all. . . . It will be a big loss if our future children never see lions."[11]

Martin interviews a number of past and current wildlife managers who are critical of hunting bans. The fundamental problem is that bans mean that the local farmers and herders see wildlife as a threat to their livelihoods. Were hunting allowed, wildlife numbers could be controlled, wild game—locally known as bushmeat—could be consumed locally or taken to market, and much less could be spent on enforcing science-based game laws than is spent on enforcing the ban.

In addition to partial or total bans, the emphasis on ecotourism entails setting aside game parks and reserves. Dowie shows how these reserves have displaced locals who have lived in or otherwise depended on utilizing the flora and fauna of the reserves, creating poverty and marginalization among formerly self-sufficient groups. (This has also occurred in the establishment of tiger reserves in India.) The hope was that the tourists would provide economic opportunities for the displaced locals. While there were jobs created in the tourist stops, they were by and large menial, low-paying ones; most of the tourist dollars were taken by the tour agencies along with the entrepreneurs who had the capital to open restaurants and hotels catering to the tourists. Little or nothing trickled down to the locals. As a consequence, the willingness of locals to put up with predation was diminished and their economic marginalization made subsistence hunting more compelling.

Perversely, the protection of wildlife, to the extent that it leads to robust populations of wildlife, makes the reserves attractive to market (bushmeat) hunters as well as heavily armed criminals who are killing elephants for their ivory, rhinos for their horns, and other animals whose body parts are valuable on the black market. The net result is that banning hunting has not been a boon to wildlife, and revenues from ecotourism have not generated adequate funding for either habitat or game management, and in effect, have increased the conflict between an expanding human population and wildlife. The result, sadly but predictably, has been that wildlife populations in Kenya have continued to decline, and in some of the reserves, wildlife populations exploded and devastated the habitat, which has led to population crashes.[12]

This said, it has to be noted that the bushmeat trade and killing of animals for their valued body parts is not simply the result of hunting bans; both bedevil all of sub-Saharan Africa. They are the result of a combination of lax enforcement (due largely to a lack of funding, but also in some instances, corruption and a lack of resolve), poverty (a rhino horn represents a sum several times larger than the typical yearly income of an African family), and a seemingly inexhaustible market, despite international bans on illegal trafficking. Risks are low and rewards are high. In countries where civil conflict is endemic, opposing forces rely on the illegal trade in wildlife to fund their military adventures. As for the bush meat trade, in many countries the need for protein is chronically unmet, and in some regions getting worse. One example will have to suffice to reveal the complexities involved in controlling the bushmeat trade. In a study of thirty years of protein consumption in Ghana, environmental science professor Justin Bradshares and colleagues found a "direct link between fish supply and subsequent bushmeat demand."[13] In recent years, European fishing fleets have begun to drive out local fishers whose traditional methods are overwhelmed by the foreign fleets. The result is the fish that ordinarily would feed Ghanaians (and other West Africans) are now feeding Europeans, causing an intensified exploitation of African wildlife for the bushmeat market.

The lion monitors are a bright spot—an indication that there are Indigenous sources of conservation that can be enlisted—but to date most of the conservation efforts have originated in Europe and North America. And as we have noted, many of the organizations that have sought to protect Africa's wildlife have been opposed to hunting (as distinct from poaching, illegally killing protected animals, or killing animals out of legal hunting times and seasons, which is universally deplored by hunters, antihunters, and agnostics alike), especially trophy hunting.

Unfortunately, trophy hunting generates significant revenues that can rival those generated by ecotourism. And the same proviso applies to both: *when properly managed*, the revenues from trophy hunting have underwritten the sustained conservation of wildlife species that otherwise would be jeopardized by illegal operations. As of this writing (2021), seven African countries permit trophy hunting of select species—South Africa, Namibia, Tanzania, Zimbabwe, Central African Republic, Burkina Faso, and Benin. Of the group, Namibia stands out; its elephant population is growing, in no small part because the revenues from trophy hunters have supported the vigorous enforcement of game laws, a science-based setting of harvest goals, and little corruption. Yet this is not the case in many other countries. For instance, Burkina Faso's wildlife reserves are currently being ravished by poachers and rebel forces.[14]

Trophy hunting, if done properly, not only generates revenues to support conservation but also addresses a need that ecotourism does not: wildlife populations need to be culled in order to reduce the inevitable conflicts between pastoralists, herders, and farmers. Africa's population is growing, and this means wildlife habitat is being inexorably encroached on, much as it was centuries ago in Europe and the West. To avoid replicating that, African nations set aside large wildlife reserves *before* their megafauna were decimated, but even large reserves cannot be sustained without culling. Cash-strapped governments can ill afford to hire and train hunters to do the culling. Affluent Westerners willing to pay for the privilege of culling makes sense—*if properly managed*—even in the face of objections to trophy hunting.

As we have seen, achieving a reasonably successful relationship between the needs of a growing population and a growing, industrialized, modern society and the nation's wildlife was no simple matter in North America or Europe. There is no reason to expect that it will be easy for other nations. Indeed, there's reason to be worried. In Africa, civil wars have weakened many new nations. Corruption is endemic, further weakening the legitimacy of central governments, and continued dependency on government loans has kept governments constantly facing austerity. And to make matters worse, trophy hunters cannot help but be reminders of colonial white supremacy. The complexity of relying on trophy hunting has recently been revealed in the controversy over the killing of a radio-collared lion in Zimbabwe that scientists had been tracking for several years and had become an attraction for ecotourists eager to observe an impressive male lion. It's not entirely clear when he acquired the name Cecil, or why he was given an English name rather than an African one, but the name stuck. As fate would have it, Cecil became more famous in death than he had been in life.

It begins with the big five: this is what African wild game hunters call those species that are the most challenging and treacherous to hunt successfully on foot. They include the lion, rhinoceros, leopard, elephant, and Cape buffalo. Whatever other mounts safari hunters may display in their trophy rooms, the most ardent—and affluent—hunters are not likely to feel their collections are complete until they have acquired souvenirs of their successfully bagging all the big five.

In 2015, Walter Palmer, an experienced hunter of African big game animals, planned a safari in Zimbabwe's Hwange National Park to add a lion to his "life list." He engaged the services of a professional hunter and local guides, and procured through them the requisite permits—a sensitive business, given the strict regulation of hunting in and around Hwange, Cecil's home territory.

Cecil was, by all accounts, an impressive lion, though at age thirteen, he was losing his grip on leading the pride. Younger males were edging him out, and that had led to his making frequent forays out of the park. Palmer's guides had strategically planted a haunch of a gazelle on private land adjacent to the park, securing permission from the private owner. Cecil came to the bait.

Palmer was hunting with a crossbow when he took the shot that wounded the lion, which ran off into the bush. Palmer and his guides tracked the wounded lion, and on finding him several days later, weakened but still very much alive, the guides dispatched Cecil with a rifle. Though Palmer no doubt would have preferred to kill the lion with a well-placed arrow, he had to have been relieved to be able to find the lion and, as the law describes it, "reduce it to possession." But whatever relief and satisfaction Palmer felt would soon evaporate.

Had Cecil not been a radio-collared research animal and something of a tourist attraction, his demise likely would have attracted little or no attention. Yet word of Cecil's death at the hands of a trophy hunter soon got out and spread quickly, fueled by the outrage of animal rights groups in Europe and the United States, the most prominent among them being the Humane Society of the United States and its sister organization, the Humane Society International.

Outraged critics demanded that Palmer be charged with alleged violations of game laws (none of the allegations were substantiated). The protests directed at Palmer were unsparing; his home and office (Palmer was a dentist) were spray-painted with graffiti denouncing him as a killer and criminal. Death threats followed, causing Palmer to temporarily close his dental practice, worried that the threats he was receiving would endanger him and his patients. Details were disseminated about Palmer's private life—that, for example, he owned a private hunting preserve—and professional practice. Yelp reviews depicted him as inept and sadistic. PETA activists called for Palmer to be publicly hanged.

The furor over the killing of Cecil was not universally shared, though. It prompted a native of Zimbabwe, Goodwell Nzou, a graduate student studying in the United States, to write an op-ed for the *New York Times* titled "In Zimbabwe, We Don't Cry for Lions." In Nzou's rural village, as in most rural villages around wildlife conservation areas, "no lion has ever been beloved, or granted an affectional nickname. They are objects of terror." Nzou told of growing up in a village prowled by a potentially human-killing lion (his uncle had been attacked by a big cat but survived). "The lion sucked the life out of the village: No one socialized by fires at night," he wrote. "No one dared stroll over to a neighbor's homestead." This lion was eventually killed, followed by rejoicing in the village. No one mourned the lion's death, nor questioned whether the hunter who killed the lion had proper documentation to do so. The stark contrast of his experience to the US and European reaction to Cecil's death led Nzou to muse, "Did all those Americans signing petitions understand that lions actually kill people? That all the talk about Cecil being 'beloved' or a 'local favorite' was media hype? Did [television show host] Jimmy Kimmel choke up because Cecil was murdered or because he confused him with Simba from 'The Lion King'?"[15]

The furor did die down, but partly in response to the "Cecil affair," the US Fish and Wildlife Service suspended the importation of trophies (the order was rescinded months later after protest from hunters and conservationists working in Africa). Several states in the United States introduced their own bans on importing trophies, but none so far have been enacted into law. A proposed ban in the United Kingdom also has been turned down in Parliament.

In contrast to how postcolonial African nations have dealt with hunting, postcolonial India has taken a different path. The long tradition of extravagant elite hunting that the British encouraged was abandoned shortly after independence. Since the 1980s, hunting has been illegal, with the exception of some birds and small game. Specific animals posing a risk to people, crops, or livestock can be killed under strict regulations, but for all practical purposes there is no sport or trophy hunting allowed.

India has gone to great lengths to protect one of its iconic animals, the Bengal tiger. It has set aside large tiger reserves, which displaced Indigenous peoples, who now live on the margins of both the reserves and, literally, society. Deprived of access to their traditional subsistence activities (such as gathering firewood), they rely on

minimal payments from the state and are regularly sub-
jected to police actions.[16] In this regard, India is replicating the experience of Africans displaced by the creation
of wildlife refuges. As in Africa, the displaced Indigenous
people scarcely benefit from ecotourists eager to see tigers.

The ban on hunting has meant that wildlife species,
many hunted to near extinction before independence, are
rebounding. That's a good thing, but, as elsewhere, not an
unmixed blessing. At the same time, India's population is
rapidly growing, and conflicts between people and wildlife have increased, especially with tigers and elephants. A
recent article in the *Guardian* reported that "1,144 people
were killed (by tigers) between April 2014 and May 2017."
In the same piece, the zoologist who directs the Wildlife
Conservation Society's program in India remarked, "We've
got tigers coming out of our ears."[17] Living in harmony with
wildlife is not a simple matter. India is trying to encourage
the people who once lived in the areas designated as tiger
reserves to move away, out of harm's way, but people are
understandably reluctant to leave the lands where their
ancestors are buried and their lifeways are rooted. People
living near the Saznekhali Wildlife Sanctuary appear to
have accepted the risks of tiger predation as the price of
maintaining their traditional lifeways, yet it is not clear
how long this tolerance will be sustained.[18] In other, less
well-managed reserves, the aforementioned *Guardian* article concluded with this observation: "Meanwhile, India's

elephants and tigers are also some of the most hunted animals in the country, sought for their ivory tusks or bones that are sold on the black market for use in traditional Chinese medicine. . . . Elephants are also threatened by speeding trains."[19] The article doesn't note that the passengers on those speeding trains might feel threatened too.

This brief examination of hunting in contemporary Europe, Africa, and India obviously glosses over many interesting variations within and between nations. The human populations in east and west Europe are declining, which might auger well for the restoration of at least some wildlife species, whether hunted or protected. But even protected species will have to be managed; the habitat needs of people along with their pets, livestock, and crops simply do not permit the unconstrained growth of all wildlife species. Too many wild boars, or too many tigers, impinge on other critters as well as people and their property. Banning sport hunting does not mean that we all suddenly inhabit a peaceable kingdom. Managing the numbers and densities of wildlife species, in all but the largest and least populated areas of Eurasia, will be necessary. In some clearly bounded areas (like islands), contraception may control numbers. In most cases, though, lethal controls will be inevitable, whether by sport hunters or trained sharpshooters and trappers.

The situation in Africa and India, and by extension, many societies, developing and developed, is becoming more dire and complex: human populations are growing, and the habitat for wildlife is shrinking. As humans and animals press closer together, conflicts mount and intensify. Add widespread poverty and robust markets for ivory, various body parts of animals large and small, and bushmeat, and even in countries where subsistence, sport, or trophy hunting is prohibited, poaching is endangering a wide swath of wildlife species. In some larger game reserves, it may be possible to rely on large carnivores to control some species of herbivores, but this is not foolproof, and with large herbivores, especially elephants, predation is nil. The last resort is starvation, which is hardly a desirable "management" strategy, yet it has been the outcome in some of Africa's game reserves, most notably Kenya's Tsavo Reserve, established in 1948. There, a burgeoning elephant population ate the herbivory to the ground, and in the late 1960s the population crashed, taking many other animals with it.[20]

If we drop the distinction between legal hunting and poaching, we could grimly conclude that hunting is flourishing in postcolonial societies, although its future is not bright. With growing human populations, the pressure on wildlife will intensify and many species will be reduced to remnant populations on heavily managed preserves, largely supported by organizations based in Europe and North America. This has already basically happened with rhinos. The preconditions for either the European model of elite-dominated hunting or the North American one of wildlife conservation simply do not exist in the postcolonial world. Indeed, there is reason to wonder about the durability of the North American model in its homeland. Living with wildlife has turned out to be a challenge everywhere that there are large human populations.

On a sunny afternoon in late September 2019, people were enjoying the day in Estes Park, Colorado. Among the attractions were a herd of twenty-some elk grazing in one of the park's meadows. People were lined up taking pictures and admiring the animals. Captured on film by Denver's CBS affiliate on September 27, a bull elk raised its head and bugled in its eerie, unmistakable mating call, and then proceeded at a stately pace toward the crowd. There were oohs and aahs, and then panic. The bull charged and knocked a woman down. Fortunately the woman was not seriously injured. Days earlier, two women were hospitalized after an encounter with another elk in another part of Estes Park. Colorado Parks and Wildlife issued a warning to the public to stay away from the elk. The elk may look peaceable as they graze, and they obviously have no fear of humans, seeming more like tame cattle than wild animals. Living with them may seem idyllic and even reassuring in the face of repeated warnings of a biodiversity crisis. As the authorities warned, however, the elk are *wild*, and not only that, September is mating season, when bulls must

bugle and strut their stuff—not to entertain the onlook-
ers, but to fend off threats to their harem and dominance.

Though the details differ—elk are not elephants, tigers, or wild boars—the challenges to the desire to replace
hunting by learning to "live with wildlife" are the same everywhere. The unchecked growth of wildlife species threat-
ens habitat, not only for themselves, but for other game
and nongame species; they also carry diseases that sicken
domestic animals and humans; they damage property
(crops, landscaping, and automobile via collisions); and
they attack livestock and/or people. Of course, few species
of wildlife pose all four threats/challenges (one, the wild
boar, is an exceptionally bad actor, which makes Monbiot's
citing them a curious example of the virtues of rewilding;
he could have celebrated the recovery of peregrine falcons,
whose major impact is on urban pigeon populations).

The success of the North American Model of Wildlife
Conservation in returning many wildlife species to sustainable populations has, for better or worse, presented
people in the United States and to a lesser extent in Canada with all four of these challenges. None involves the
dire choices facing many sub-Saharan African nations—
extinction is not, for the foreseeable future, an issue with
North American game species—but accommodating these
now-robust wildlife species is nevertheless fast becoming
a serious challenge—and one made more vexing because
it is no longer clear that sport hunters by themselves can

be effective "management tools." We will have much more to say about this in the concluding chapter. For now, we will look at several species whose abundance has divided the public over how to live with wildlife. There are a number of species whose increasing numbers create conflicts, such as beavers for example.[21] Still, since we are concerned with hunting, we will focus on three species that hunters have played a decisive role in promoting: white-tailed deer, Canada and snow geese, and wild turkeys.[22] We'll begin with the white-tailed deer, the animal that attracts the largest percentage of hunters nationwide.

White-Tailed Deer

Scarce in the first half of the twentieth century, white-tailed deer have become so numerous that they are severely altering the ecology of forests from coast to coast. In a word, they are simplifying forests, suppressing the regeneration of those species in the herbivory that they feed on. In the Northeast, the result is a forest of mature trees with the forest's floor a sweeping carpet of ferns. To the unsuspecting observer, the scene looks lush—a forest primeval. It is anything but. The deer browse all the seedlings and brushy plants on which invertebrates depend, and that means that birds and small mammals who depend on the invertebrates disappear. It also means that the affected forests are more vulnerable to storm events and disease. Simplified systems are less resilient; even when the deer density declines, there is no guarantee that the original ensemble of species will return. Indeed, the evidence is piling up that some impacts of deer may be irreversible.[23]

The explosive growth of the deer population in the past forty years is the result of several interacting factors, some intentional and others not. As we saw earlier, state wildlife agencies began setting regulations in the late nineteenth and early twentieth centuries that were designed to promote the recovery of deer. Seasons when deer could legally be hunted were set to protect deer during their breeding time (known as the rut), bag limits were established, and most important, does were protected. (Under most circumstances, only bucks were legal.) As long as a few bucks survived the hunting season, the bucks could impregnate the abundant does and they would deliver fawns in the spring, and thus the herd would grow.

In addition to deliberate efforts to boost the deer population, the steady decline of small farms over the course of the past century has led to fields returning to forest—a plethora of young trees all within easy browse heights for deer. And when those young forests started to be turned into new subdivisions and shopping malls, the edges separating cul-de-sacs from one another, along with the open spaces devoted to future development or local parks, provided attractive habitat for deer. At the same time, hunting regulations promulgated early in the twentieth century that were designed to increase historically low deer numbers were slow to change in the face of increasing numbers of deer. Quite apart from the "bucks only" regulations, the culture of deer hunting had long been oriented to getting a buck. Where permitted, hunters could kill one doe "for the camp," " but the real hunt was for bucks, preferably specimens with impressive antlers. Bucks are more elusive, and older bucks are especially wary, having survived several seasons of being hunted. Killing a large buck with impressive antlers was and is regarded as an enviable accomplishment—a testament to a hunter's skill. When agency goals shifted toward population *control*, agencies sought to encourage killing does since their numbers were the key to population control. Yet many hunters resisted the invitation. The common opposition was compelling because it was true: "kill a doe and you kill two deer (one living and one to be born in the spring), kill a buck and you kill one deer." Hunters understandably preferred more, not fewer, deer. Those charged with managing deer herds walked a tightrope between trying to mitigate the problems of deer density and the hunters' (whose hunting licenses funded state wildlife agencies) demand for more deer. Some states with particularly high deer densities have experimented with requiring hunters to first kill a doe before they can hunt for a buck. As of this writing, no "best practice" standard has emerged, and deer continue to multiply. Along with that, problems have multiplied.

Deer also have an economic impact on orchards and crops. A study conducted by researchers at the Cornell Cooperative Extension estimated that deer annually cause $100 million in crop damage, $750 million in timber losses, and $250 million in damage to household landscaping and gardening in New York state alone.[24] In recent years, collisions between deer and cars have caused at least $4 billion a year in vehicle damage, several hundred deaths each year, and untold nonfatal injuries, not to mention injuring and killing many deer.

In many suburbs, living with deer has meant living with Lyme disease. The Centers for Disease Control and Prevention estimates that there are likely as many as three hundred thousand new cases of Lyme disease each year, and in some heavily deer-impacted areas, Lyme disease has become a virtual epidemic. Lyme is only one of the tick-borne diseases associated with high deer densities. In a particularly ironic twist, a newly reported disease transmitted by the lone star tick (whose range is spreading from the Southwest to the Midwest and East Coast) creates a severe allergic reaction in some bite victims to the consumption of red meat.

High deer density is not good for deer either. Deer are vectors of Lyme and other tick-borne diseases. Though they are not affected themselves, they are grievously impacted by chronic wasting disease, a prion-caused illness like mad cow disease. It attacks the central nervous system of the infected animal, causing it to grow progressively disoriented. It is a highly contagious and 100 percent fatal disease. The chronic wasting disease first emerged in the confined deer and elk herds in Colorado in the mid-twentieth century. It is persistent in the environment, and there is no known cure or eradication protocol. As of 2020, it has been found in twenty-three US states and two western provinces in Canada as well as in reindeer and moose in Norway and moose in Finland. Many states have begun to prohibit bringing unbutchered deer across state lines, as the spine, brains, and internal organs, but apparently not the meat, are suspected reservoirs of the prion. So far there is no evidence of a human made ill by the consumption of venison properly cared for.

In recent decades, many cities have been the scene of bitter conflicts between those who want deer numbers sharply reduced and those who enjoy seeing deer in their yards and parks. Underscoring poet Robert Frost's ironic line that "good fences make good neighbors," the fences popping up in neighborhoods across the country suggest a breakdown in neighborliness. Laws prohibiting the deliberate feeding of deer are increasingly common and exacerbate tensions between neighbors. Living with deer is, to say the least, a challenge.

Geese

The North American population of Canada geese has been undergoing a transformation that amounts to speciation— the division of one species into two. Some portion of the total population continues to migrate each spring to northern breeding grounds and then in fall to warmer climes in the south. But an increasing number have lost interest in long-distance migrations. This started in the nineteenth century when market hunters and sportsmen captured geese, and tethered them in fields and ponds to attract their migratory cousins. Bred in captivity, it didn't take many generations for the geese to bond to the places where they were born. When, in the 1930s, the use of live decoys was outlawed as unsportsmanlike, thousands of captive geese were released in the hopes that they would bolster the lagging population of wild Canadas.[25] The expansion of office parks with their obligatory aerated ponds and green swards, suburban golf courses and city parks, not to mention climate change, which has kept more and more rivers and lakes from freezing over, have made growing numbers of "Canada" geese year-round residents. The result is that parks and golf courses where the geese feed, and urban lakes and ponds where geese roost, are carpeted in goose droppings. At best, this creates a nuisance; at worst, it's a public health hazard. New York City spends over $1 million a year keeping geese from contaminating the reservoirs that are the city's drinking water.

Despite this, as with deer, geese have supporters who in case after case vigorously oppose efforts to reduce the nonmigratory goose numbers. Much like the conflict over deer management, proposals to round up geese and send them off to be killed—their meat donated to food banks, and their feathers sold for fashionable pillows and down jackets—are routinely met with protests from animal rights groups and locals who enjoy the presence of the impressive birds. Sharing the landscape with what amounts to partly tame exemplars of "the wild" is reassuring, conjuring a pastoral ideal that is comforting, despite the feces in the case of geese, and the landscaping damage and collisions in the case of deer.

States have set up separate hunting seasons for nonmigratory geese that begin before the migrations starts and end once the migrants from the breeding areas in the far north begin moving south. But as with deer, some of the greatest densities occur in places where hunting is unsafe or too offensive to the nonhunting population. For hunters' part, it's hard to imagine them eager to put their blinds near the ninth hole of a country club golf course, much less on the shore of a pond in an office park. So the nonmigratory population continues to grow, even as the population of the migratory geese fluctuates around a slowly declining trend. As of this writing (2021), the daily limit on migratory geese in Maryland has been cut from two birds per day to one. Maryland's Eastern Shore has long been the epicenter of wintering Canada geese, and goose hunting has long been a major feature of the region's culture and economy.

While the population of migratory Canada geese is at least temporarily in decline, another species, the snow goose, is booming. Along its three major flyways—the Pacific, Mississippi, and Atlantic—literal clouds of thousands of snow geese can be seen rising from fields where they have been feeding or bodies of water where they have been roosting. Snow geese are more difficult to hunt than Canada geese; a huge number of decoys are required to even have a chance of luring them within gun range, and they are more difficult to call. Jan has sat in blinds in both the Atlantic and Pacific flyways, and seen flocks of two and three thousand fly overhead, well out of range, paying no attention to the decoys or calls, while Canadas flying at lower elevations will, more obligingly, at least circle temptingly over the decoys, checking things out—and sometimes decide to set their wings so as to descend to join the decoys and come within shooting range. In over twenty years of goose hunting, Jan has never seen a snow goose within shooting range.

Most goose hunters prefer to shoot the iconic Canada goose. Hunters who specialize in snow geese are a resolute bunch, but their skills have been no match for the wiliness and fecundity of the geese. Their numbers are scarcely impacted, even though state and federal agencies have relaxed the regulations on hunting snow geese. For example, waterfowl hunters are required to use shotguns that are limited to holding no more than three shells (a standard semiautomatic or pump shotgun holds up to five shells). This diminishes the temptation to blast away at a flight of birds. But in some states, hunters are legally able to modify their shotguns to hold as many as ten shells when hunting snow geese. On the Eastern Shore of Maryland, the daily limit in the 2019–2020 season was one Canada goose, yet the daily limit on snow geese was twenty! Electronic calls (amplified recordings of geese) are illegal, except in some states, where they can be used when hunting snow geese.

The reason for encouraging killing lots of snow geese is that their huge flocks are having a ruinous impact on the fragile northern breeding grounds that are crucial for ducks, Canada geese, and all sorts of nongame migratory species. Not only are they hogging the food supply, their aggressive feeding is diminishing the regeneration of the grasses in the fragile ecosystems of the arctic north. In effect, they are the winged equivalent of deer. Eventually the population will exceed the regenerative capacity of the arctic breeding habitat and the snow geese population will crash. But lots of other species will go down with the metaphoric ship. And as with deer impacts, recovery of the breeding grounds, once the snow geese numbers decrease significantly, is by no means assured. Given all the other stresses that migratory birds, game, and nongame alike face, compromised breeding grounds can have devastating effects on the populations of species. It seems that draconian—and inevitably controversial—measures will need to be taken to save habitat vital to sustaining viable populations of migratory birds.

Wild Turkeys

On a lighter note, let us conclude with one of the most successful wildlife recoveries entirely attributed to hunters along with the federal and state agencies that hunters support. It did not take long for the colonists to hunt the wild turkey, which polymath Benjamin Franklin thought should be named the "American bird," to local extinction in the New England colonies. The extirpation continued as settlers moved westward. From an estimated population of 10 million when Europeans arrived on America's shores, by 1920 it was estimated that there were no more than 30,000 of the big birds left, largely concentrated in South Carolina and Missouri. There were several unsuccessful attempts to capture wild birds and release them in areas where biologists thought they could thrive. Improvements in capture technology and the identification of wild populations free of genetic traces of domesticated turkeys led to successful capture and relocations. The National Wild Turkey Federation was founded in 1973, by which time there were an estimated 1.3 million wild turkeys. The federation pursued its own restocking program, and by 2001 there were an estimated 5.5 million birds and as many as 2.6 million hunters pursuing them. There are now huntable wild turkey populations in all states except Alaska and even in states where turkeys were not native (Hawaii).[26]

Flocks of turkeys disrupt traffic, and aggressive toms have been known to attack reflections of themselves in windows and the side panels of shiny new automobiles. In one subdivision in a southeastern Massachusetts town, a large territorial tom repeatedly attacked a mail carrier, who ultimately refused to deliver the mail—rain, sleet, and snow, but no turkey.

Of course, there are other wildlife species that now create headaches for the state agencies on which we depend to manage wildlife. Beaver, black and brown (grizzly) bears, wolves, urban and suburban elk, and mountain lions come readily to mind. We've chosen three species that hunters have played a significant role in promoting and thus can be said to bear some responsibility in figuring out how to cope with an abundance that no one could have predicted when the North American Model of Wildlife Conservation was first promoted. Indeed, who could have imagined geese overrunning a city park, deer becoming a major factor in determining what grows in our suburban backyards, or turkeys interrupting mail deliveries.

Part of what encourages conflicts between wildlife and people is that having deprived wildlife of unlimited habitat, more and more species have learned to live with us faster than we have learned to live with them. And when we begin to share the same spaces, the essential ingredient of their wildness—fear of us—dissipates. To be sure, they are still "wild," but because they are not as threatened by us, they wind up being pests, nuisances, and occasionally, menacing. Those who celebrate rewilding yet oppose lethal control, whether by hunters or licensed exterminators (animal control services), are in effect redefining what it means to be wild. So deer are dubbed "horned rats" and Canada geese get labeled "lawn carp." (We haven't yet heard of a similar renaming of turkeys, but it's no doubt on its way.) From a hunter's perspective, suburban deer and golf course geese are degraded versions of the real—the wild and elusive thing. To the extent that wildness is genetically hardwired, it's because the species has evolved in response to being hunted. Absent hunting pressure, deer, geese, and turkeys lose their fear of humans. So do bears, coyotes, and mountain lions.[77]

The implicit assumption that informs the "living with wildlife" program is that it is not only desirable to end hunting but practical to do so as well. We can learn to get along with one another. There is no doubt that we could be

Having deprived wildlife of unlimited habitat, more and more species have learned to live with us faster than we have learned to live with them.

more accommodating to the needs of wildlife—for example, by not encroaching on their habitat. Yet that "simple" measure has a whole host of implications that in the aggregate, constitute a radical realignment of how we behave, starting with drastic reductions in the rates of our population growth, consumption of natural resources, creation of literal mountains of trash, and pollution of land and water, just for starters. The course we are on means that clashes with wildlife are inevitable, and as important, it means that some wild animal populations will need to be controlled, not only for our benefit, but for the benefit of those species that suffer when deer or geese take over an area as well as the overabundant deer or geese. From the animal's point of view, it doesn't matter whether its death is at the hands of a sport hunter or hired sharpshooter. But should it matter to us? It's to this and related questions that we now turn as we contemplate the future of hunting.

CONTINUITIES AND CONTINGENCIES

Hunting in the Twenty-First Century

For all the variations across time and cultures, some features of the hunt appear to recur. If not universal, these features are common enough in our current debates over hunting as descendants of the ways hunting even in the remote past was symbolically loaded. Of course, hunting has changed dramatically over time, but the anxieties aroused by killing wild animals have a lengthy history. In this, the concluding chapter, our historical review will frame our discussion of the challenges facing hunters and hunting in the twenty-first century. But before turning to the future, let's briefly review the recurring features of hunting.

Males predominated, though not all males hunted. Some males had no appetite for the hunt or lost the desire to hunt. Others could no longer meet the physical demands. As a result, at any moment in time only a minority of any population hunted. Though a majority of

For all the variations across time and cultures, some features of the hunt appear to recur.

those who hunted were male, in both myth and life, some women hunted or were integral to the hunt, if not directly engaged in the kill. With few exceptions in the modern era, when professional hunters emerged, hunters hunted episodically. It was not a full-time job, and as we have seen, Stone Age hunters rarely produced more than a small percentage of the calories needed to feed the group or family. There are of course exceptions. Circumpolar peoples were heavily dependent on fish, marine animals, and caribou. Given short growing seasons, plants were a small proportion of their diet. And the Plains Indians were heavily dependent on bison.

The killing of animals, especially large, warm-blooded ones, triggered a volatile mix of emotions that yielded normative practices that absolved the hunter of guilt or remorse—sentiments that could otherwise make the hunter hesitant to kill. Preparations for the hunt often involved seeking the approval of one or another god or goddess or a village seer. Just as our ancestors had rituals to seek blessings for the planting of crops and giving thanks for the harvest, so too did hunting generate its own rich myth and lore, elements of which persist, albeit in more secular garb, down to the present.

The fact that hunters, then and now, take pleasure in hunting and find satisfaction in a successful kill has been, and continues to be, the basis for a critique of hunters and hunting more generally. Greek philosophers worried about the suffering of animals and character of those who imposed the suffering. Philosopher Jeremy Bentham millennia later decried the suffering of animals. And in our own day, philosophers including Peter Singer and Thomas Regan, while disagreeing on important matters, each came to the conclusion that hunting, especially sport hunting, should be ended. And as we have seen, some critics go one step further to claim that hunting attracts bad characters, or makes otherwise normal people callous and cruel.

Finally, once states and empires began to emerge, hunting and combat became associated with one another. The skills of the hunter were more or less easily adapted to those needed in combat. Tactics were transferable too, from ambush to direct face-to-face attack. Indeed, as we have seen, royal hunts frequently mobilized hundreds of "troops" to drive game to the waiting hunters. It took a long time, but we've gone from war chariots enlisted in hunting down lions to all-terrain vehicles to get hunters into the field. Long bows are now replaced by a bow made of a complex combination of graphite, pulleys, and high-tech strings of polyester. Muskets have been replaced by high-powered rifles, some of which are now computer driven with deadly accuracy up to 1,000 to 1,500 yards (there are 1,760 yards in a *mile*). The ATVs and compound bows are the result of ordinary marketing and human ingenuity. The modern rifle and optics that make it so deadly have been largely the result of the desire of states and empires to produce more effective weapons of war. These improvements then find their way into the civilian market with modifications suitable for hunting rather than combat. A fully equipped contemporary archer or rifle hunter more closely resembles a member of a swat team than they do frontiersman Davy Crockett or Teddy Roosevelt.

As the preceding chapters have made clear, the changes over long stretches of time can be made to appear linear, much as the story of our species' evolution, which we described at the outset of this volume, made our career appear linear, foreordained by evolutionary forces. But as we hope we've demonstrated, continuities are punctuated by contingency. After all, if evolution had selected men to be violent, a proposition we do not accept, we would not have to go to lengths to prepare men for battle, there would be no male objectors to war, and instead of facing a dramatic decline in the number of male hunters in the United States and Europe, we would expect to see the woods teeming with men in pursuit of game. This is not to deny the power of evolutionary selection, or dimorphism of male and female; it is to say that even characteristics that seem hardwired like sexual dimorphism, are in fact contingent on cultural forces that shape our "raw material" into attitudes and behavior that are deemed acceptable to the group(s) with which we associate. To appreciate this, let us pick up where we left off in chapter 4 portraying the rapid decline in the number of hunters that began in the 1980s, both here and in Europe.

In the United States, the declines in hunting participation have been most dramatic in the Northeast and on the Pacific Coast. It might not be surprising to learn that the numbers of hunters have declined in heavily settled Connecticut, Rhode Island, or Massachusetts, but it is surprising, at least to those who worry about the future of hunting, to see the numbers drop almost as precipitously in still largely rural Vermont, New Hampshire, and Maine. In California, there were 700,000 hunting licenses sold in 1970. Forty-nine years later, after the population had roughly doubled, only 225,000 licenses were purchased.[1] Oregon and Washington State have seen similar declines. According to a recent report by the Federation of Associations for Hunting and Conservation of the European Union, the same is true for the European Union. In the thirty-six countries involved, only 1 to 2 percent of the adult population hunts.[2]

Hunting remains more popular in the Mountain States, upper Midwest, and the South, but even there the number of hunters is declining. We've already discussed the multiple reasons for this, so we need not repeat them here, but to underline the contingencies involved in this decline, we need to add an important wrinkle to the data. The decline would be even steeper but for the fact that the number of women becoming hunters has been increasing in recent decades. The latest data indicate that women now constitute 10 percent of the nation's hunters. In the European Union, the Federation of Associations for Hunting and Conservation reports that women constitute 7 percent of the European Union's hunters.[3] What's going on?

The obvious answer is that the revolution in gender relations begun in the 1960s has literally liberated women to challenge the norms that created and sustained a sexual division in what was appropriate for men versus women. In a historic "wink of the eye," women started running marathons, playing soccer and ice hockey, and winning Olympic competitions in shooting sports, and they now constitute the majority of law, medical, and veterinary school graduates. Men still predominate in the ranks of hunters, but if the present trends continue, it won't be long before women decked out in camo or blaze orange will become commonplace.

These remarkable changes did not just happen. It took a women's movement to challenge the array of stereotypes and legal impediments to women's equality. So it is with attracting women to hunting. For a long time, the few women drawn to hunting were encouraged by their husbands or boyfriends. But that has changed too; the socialization can just as readily be carried out by female-friendly hunting skills workshops, most notably the Becoming an Outdoors-Woman program, founded in 1991 by Christine Thomas and her colleagues in the environmental studies program at the University of Wisconsin at Stevens Point, and currently operating in forty-nine US states, five Canadian provinces, and New Zealand. Over a quarter million women have participated in one or more Becoming an Outdoors-Woman's workshops. They tend to be college educated, more urban, of moderate to high household income, and in the thirty-five to fifty-five age range, much like the males who are deciding to begin hunting in adulthood.

Another contender for female attention and participation is the National Wildlife Federation's Artemis Sportswomen program. This recently founded initiative is particularly significant in that unlike Becoming an Outdoors-Woman, which is funded primarily through state wildlife agencies, Artemis Sportswomen is privately funded by a prominent organization known for its support of conservation and environmental policies. It is the first time such an entity has been willing to throw some serious money at a female-focused program.

Significantly, then, the divide between hunter/conservationist and green/environmentalist that characterized the twentieth-century debate is less pronounced among women as a group. Female hunters therefore offer new, constructive models for envisioning environmental sustainability. Years of researching the ideas and motivations of female hunters suggest convincingly that as a group, women think through the meaning of their outdoor life in ways that help lend deeper and potentially more coherent meaning to the phrase "hunter-environmentalist." These women are, intentionally or not, rewriting the story we humans like to tell about ourselves. Female hunters and environmental activists—and there are many women who are both—have a key role to play in the dialogue that we as a global society desperately need to commence about what it means to live in this ever more imperiled natural world, as very human animals. Artemis—the Roman Diana—was the goddess of both hunting and childbirth. The simple fact that the hand that rocks the cradle can also wield a 30-06 rifle should tell us something, and not just about the shifting demographics of hunting *or* changing circumstances of women's lives. Women's hunting forces us—men and women, hunters and nonhunters alike—to rethink our relationship to and responsibility for the nonhuman world in some fresh, provocative, and constructive ways.

There is another contingency at work that has so far had less effect on the total number of hunters, but has had an interesting effect on the demography of them. As we have seen, there has been a steady decline in the recruitment of young boys, yet as we've noted, there has been an uptick in the recruitment of young adult males and females in their twenties and thirties—a phenomenon that author Tovar Cerulli has dubbed "adult-onset hunters."[4] He is himself a specimen, moving from an adolescent vegan to an adult "mindful carnivore." Cerulli also suggests that adult-onset hunters bring a more fully developed ethical sensibility to the hunt than most young adolescent males. Whether it's testosterone or the immature need to dominate, hunter education instructors almost universally report that adolescent males are their most difficult students. These students come into the program thinking that they already know everything. By contrast, girls and young adult men and women are more accepting of being novices in need of instruction. (This difference between young boys and young girls as well as young adults of both sexes is also reflected in differences in auto insurance since adolescent boys have more accidents than girls as well as young men and women.) The decline in adolescent recruits may, in this sense, not be as much of a problem for the future of hunting as long as this decline continues to be offset by adult-onset hunters. The maturity of hunters may compensate for the quantity of them.

This said, there was a departure from the decline in hunters in 2020. Across the country, the sales of hunting licenses in the forty-four states reporting thus far increased by 5 percent. The increase varied across regions, but increased even in the Northeast and Pacific States—regions that have experienced the sharpest declines in recent years.[5] Enrollment in hunter education courses also appears to have increased, indicating that many of these license buyers were first-time hunters. In all likelihood, this was a response to the COVID-19 pandemic. Many workers were laid off, children were being remotely schooled, and many forms of entertainment—sporting events, concerts, and large family gatherings—were suspended. And people were urged to recreate outdoors. It remains to be seen if this uptick marks a sustained reversal of the decline in hunting or just a short-lived response to the pandemic.

Not all the contingencies facing the future of hunting are as encouraging as the growth of young adult men and women interested in hunting. For reasons we examined in chapter 4, we think broad social changes will continue to depress the total number of hunters, particularly in the United States. The desire to hunt is not inborn, much less limited to men, but to sustain the desire, there has to be reasonable access to the opportunity to hunt. When access is limited, numbers will not only be low but also largely made up of people, male and female, who can afford to pay for access to private hunting reserves, hunting clubs, or hired outfitters and guides. This has been the case for generations, with national variations across England and the Continent. But as we've seen, the United States and Canada produced a different model that basically assured access to anyone who legally acquired a license to hunt, and abided by the laws regulating hunting seasons and bag limits. Hunters enjoyed open access to large swaths of public lands, federal wildlife refuges, and especially in the Northeast and upper Midwest, a large percentage of private lands that were not explicitly "posted"—signs at the property boundaries declaring "No Trespassing" or "No Hunting."

Suburban sprawl has sharply reduced areas near population centers that were once open to hunters. And in recent decades as urbanites, untethered from offices and freed by telecommuting, moved onto former small farms and woodlots, the "No Trespassing" signs burgeoned in rural areas. (To be fair, some of these ex-urbanites were drawn to hunting, but they generally regard, as is their legal right, their property as off-limits to other hunters.) The net result is that there has been a steady decline in lands suitable for hunting, particularly land that is near population centers. That has meant that hunters have been forced to travel farther to find hunting opportunities. This poses several different ways that diminish hunter interest. One is simply financial. Travel costs money and time. Yet that may not be determinative by itself. A significant pleasure that hunters derive from hunting is familiarity with favorite places that drip with memories, such as where dad first took me along, where I got my first buck, where my puppy made its first polished retrieve of a pheasant or duck. Hunters are sentimentalists—remember the cave paintings—and regularly exchange tales with one another of memorable hunts. Their hearts sink when they see a favorite spot festooned with surveyor's flags. In the face of such assaults on memories, some hunters simply quit hunting. In his study of hunters in Massachusetts, Jan also encountered hunters whose interest in hunting was waning because their children were either uninterested in or opposed to hunting, or opposed to eating game.[6]

The loss of familiar places has coincided with the aging of the postwar generation of hunters (World War II, Korea, and Vietnam), who are now becoming "aging adult former hunters." Outdoors writer David E. Petzal, the firearms editor for *Field and Stream*, writes of a reader's email, in which they explained, "I've been a serious hunter of all of my 61 years. I've chased virtually every game species in the Western U.S. and Alaska. But I have a problem. Over the past couple of years, I've had trouble pulling the trigger. Mechanically, I'm fine. Mentally, not so much. I just don't enjoy the killing part anymore. What the hell is wrong with me?" Petzal responds, saying that he hunts less too, and goes on to say that many aging, but not *aged*, hunters also experience a declining interest in the kill.[7]

Aldo Leopold famously observed his "trigger itch" as a young Forest Service employee, implicitly suggesting that as a mature adult, he no longer was intent on shooting at every opportunity. Social ecology professor Stephen Kellert also observed this same phenomenon in his widely regarded study of hunters' motivations.[8] Getting into the woods may still be compelling and seeing game remains thrilling, but the desire to kill the pheasant or deer just isn't important anymore. (It should be noted that some number of hunters continue to buy hunting licenses to support state agencies, even though they no longer hunt.)

Hunting in unfamiliar places imposes its own challenges. Unfamiliarity requires time to scout for productive covers and get familiar with property boundaries as well as the location of houses, outbuildings, and pastures with livestock. It helps to introduce yourself to the landowner(s). All of this can be rewarding, and the anecdotal evidence is that deep bonds have been forged between landowners and hunters who sometimes travel a thousand miles or more to find new hunting grounds. Still, the fact remains that losing familiar hunting covers or facing hurdles to access new covers is one of the reasons adult hunters give for putting their guns and bows away.

Public lands are also under pressure. In the East, public lands are relatively small, especially state-owned lands, and crowded. They remain popular because the state fish and game agencies typically release pheasants, and in some states quail, because there otherwise would be too few or no wild birds to make hunting attractive. Again, if given a choice, most hunters would prefer wild birds and wide-open spaces, but that's not a choice for more and more hunters. State agencies depend heavily on the sales of hunting licenses, so they have to release pen-raised birds to keep hunters buying licenses.

In the West, the retention of hunters is a problem too, yet for different reasons. One problem arises from the fact that more and more hunters are traveling farther and farther to find promising hunting opportunities. Typically, these nonresident hunters will hire guides and outfitters who have made arrangements with local ranchers so that their clients have exclusive access for hunts varying from a couple of days to a couple of weeks, depending on the depths of the hunters' pockets. These nonresident hunters pay significantly higher license fees, and bring in revenues to rural areas that can turn a rancher's bottom line from red or pink to black. But this is having the effect of removing some of the most productive hunting from local hunters. In Montana, for example, the number of resident hunters has been declining while the number of nonresident ones has been increasing.[9] A recent study reported that "more and more . . . [Montana] hunters are expressing frustration that hunting is turning into a game of 'haves' and 'have-nots.'"[10]

While the notion that nonresident hunters are all rich is wrong, it is true that some ranchers have marketed themselves for the wealthy. Entrepreneur Ted Turner is, to say the least, not typical, but nevertheless exemplifies what locals complain about. Turner has bought up a number of huge, noncontiguous ranches. He was until recently the largest individual (noninstitutional) landowner in the United States. Turner has invested in restoring his holdings to their ecological condition before cattle, replacing cows with bison. It's a vast ecological restoration project that is, on its own terms, a worthy environmental gift to posterity. He has restored riverine habitats degraded by cattle that now boast healthy, sustainable populations of native trout species as well as elk, mule deer, and antelope. For a five-figure fee, a hunter can enjoy a week of hunting and fishing on one or another of Turner's several ranches.[11] As praiseworthy as Turner's efforts to restore degraded lands to their former vitality and species diversity are, he is also an illustration of the process by which access to hunting opportunities is becoming increasingly commercialized—the antithesis of one of the fundamental pillars of the North American Model of Wildlife Conservation.

To respond to this loss of access, a number of states have promoted programs that pay or reduce tax rates for landowners who improve their land for game in exchange for agreeing to keep their land open to public hunting. But the growth of commercialized access has been inexorable in recent decades. Deprived of access to traditional hunting grounds and pressed for time, more and more hunters are paying guides to arrange access, joining hunting preserves where game birds are released, or paying for hunting on ranches boasting exotic animals or deer that have been bred to have impressive antlers. As we've seen, commercialized hunting in the nineteenth century devastated the nation's game populations. Today's commercialization may, ironically, take pressure off wild game, although it arguably reduces hunters' interest in supporting the organizations that have played a large role in promoting wildlife habitat. Commercialization also risks diminishing the experience of the hunt. Having purchased six pheasants and thus knowing they are in a specified area, the engagement with the bird is altered; in effect, it's hard not to think of the birds as "mine." After all, the hunter paid for them. As any hunter will confess, pen-raised birds are not the same as wild ones. Wild birds know where they are—and hence where the best escape routes and thick, protective cover can be gotten to, or when to fly and when to hold tight. Pen-raised birds are not unintelligent; they are not like domesticated chickens. They do their best to elude the hunter and are often successful. They challenge the hunter's shooting skills and the hunter's dog, but the chase lacks the edge that the search for a wild bird entails. The same goes for farmed deer and elk.

Commercialization may in the long run ensure a stable, if narrower, base for hunting, making hunting in the United States more like hunting in Europe. The result will be a challenge for state wildlife agencies whose existence depends heavily on license sales. Declining license sales have already forced some state agencies to cut back on programs. It bears repeating that the restoration and continued support of wildlife, both game and nongame, has been largely accomplished by the state agencies funded by hunters, directly and indirectly.

There is one other recent development involving access to hunting opportunities that bears mention. It is a development that Canadian and US hunters both face: public lands, particularly in the western states and provinces, are under pressure from extractive industries, whether for forest products or fossil fuel (coal, tar sands, oil, and fracked gas), or mining for copper, uranium, and other metals. In the United States, federally owned forests and land, overseen by the US Forest Service and Bureau of Land Management (BLM), respectively, are charged with promoting a policy of "multiple use." The Forest Service authorizes the building of roads to facilitate approved timber harvests. The BLM leases grazing rights to people who tend or raise cattle, and grants permits to mine and extract oil and natural gas. There has been a long history of conflict over these permits and leases. Conservationists initially supported the policy of multiple use, but in the late 1940s, many in the conservation movement lobbied Congress to enact legislation to set aside large tracts of public land, again mostly in the western states, and declare them "wilderness." Prominent individuals in the second generation of conservationists (including Leopold, Forest Service chief of recreation and lands Bob Marshall, Alaska Conservation Society founder Celia Hunter, renowned photographer Ansel Adams, and Mardy Murie, who was instrumental in getting the Alaska National Wildlife Refuge established) were responsible for the passage of the Wilderness Act in 1964. Written by Wilderness Society member Howard Zahniser, the act famously stipulates that "a wilderness, in contrast with those areas where man and his works dominate the landscape, is hereby recognized as an area where the earth and its community of life are untrammeled by man, where man himself is a visitor who does not remain."[17]

This act removed large tracts of land from the multiple use policy and ironically may have spurred what came to be known as the Sagebrush Rebellion, also referred to as the wise use movement. The landmark environmental acts of the early 1970s contributed to the conservative reaction too. The rebellion/movement was launched by conservatives in the western states who resented federal control over large chunks of land within their borders. To take two extreme examples, 84 percent of the landmass of Nevada is federal land; in Utah, 65 percent of the landmass is under federal control. Initially funded by the conservative beer magnate Joseph Coors, the rebellion focused largely on opposition to environmental regulations that erected barriers to resource extraction on federal lands. Coors and other wealthy western conservatives formed the Mountain State Legal Foundation (1974), which began a series of lawsuits challenging federal policies. When Ronald Reagan took office as US president in 1981, he named James Watt, a lawyer for the Mountain State Legal Foundation, as his secretary of the interior and Ann Gorsuch (mother of then president Donald J. Trump's appointment to the US Supreme Court, Neil Gorsuch) to head the Environmental Protection Agency. Another man associated with the Sagebrush Rebellion, politician Robert Burford, was named as head of the BLM. All three left office under clouds of mismanagement, and in Burford's case, self-dealing.

The movement died down after these embarrassing departures, but it did not go away. It has resurfaced in recent decades with the discovery of large coal deposits and shale gas. The clamor for exploiting these resources to enrich local and state governments was one of the rallying cries. With the election of Trump in 2016, the movement once again had a sympathetic president who appointed heads of the US Forest Service, Department of the Interior, and BLM who, in turn, set about adopting policies that promoted resource extraction on public lands. In an unprecedented move, President Trump ordered a substantial reduction of several national monuments, notably Bears Ears and the Grand Staircase-Escalante National Monuments, thereby opening these large tracts to mining and oil and gas exploration.

Many of these initiatives are being challenged in the courts by environmental groups and Native American tribes whose ancestral lands are contained in the desig-nated monuments, but should these challenges be denied, hunters and outdoor enthusiasts will face public lands that will be fragmented as well as dotted with the detritus of oil rigs, spent mines, and the roads that service them for decades to come. More than aesthetics are involved, though. These developments are also having negative im-pacts on wildlife, disrupting traditional migration routes, polluting watercourses, and reducing breeding habitats for both game and nongame birds and animals.

Taken together, all of these trends will contribute to dis-courage active hunters, who will then hunt less or give up entirely. We predict it will also make the recruitment of first-time hunters more difficult, although we are less cer-tain about this latter effect. The reason that new hunters may be easier to recruit than older ones are to be retained is due to the phenomenon of "shifting baselines." Biolo-gists have begun using the phrase to describe how each generation accepts conditions as they find them, without realizing that they are experiencing a deteriorating condi-tion. This process was dramatically demonstrated by Loren McClenachan, a graduate student who discovered a series of pictures taken of fishers using the same fishing char-ter in Key West, Florida, starting in 1947. In the earliest photo, the sports, two men and a woman, were grinning broadly alongside their catch of the day, giant grouper and several sharks, some of which were almost as big as the anglers. In successive photos, the scene was repeated: smiling anglers alongside fish, but with each successive photo, the fish were smaller and less numerous. The most recent photos taken in the early 2000s show "small snapper, which once weren't deemed worthy of a photo; people just piled them on the dock."[13]

Put simply, new hunters have nothing to compare to current conditions. Hunting pen-raised birds is exciting—the dog work is fun to watch, the shooting is challenging enough to assure hunters that they are not shooting "ducks on a pond," and the birds are not quite as bland as mass-produced chicken. But something important gets lost when the game being pursued is not quite wild, in the full sense of the word. Moreover, commercial hunting preserves have invited opponents of hunting to decry "canned hunts."

Recruitment to hunting, whether of youngsters or adults, depends on more than access to good places to hunt that are broadly affordable. It also requires that the nonhunting public not only approve of hunting but also think well of hunters. From the beginning of this book, we've discussed the ambivalence with which nonhunters have regarded hunters. There's something of a paradox involved here. Recent research has shown that a large majority of people in the United States approve of "legal hunting" and hunting for food. Yet this drops off quite

Recruitment to hunting,
whether of youngsters
or adults, depends on
more than access to
good places to hunt that
are broadly affordable.

dramatically when respondents are asked if they approve of "sport hunting," and it drops even more dramatically when asked if they approve of "trophy hunting." Here is the summary of the report:

> Overall, 80% of Americans approve of legal hunting. Approval of hunting is highest in the Midwest (at 86% approval) and is lowest in the Northeast (72%). Americans' level of approval of hunting has remained generally consistent over the past quarter century, with a gradual increase in approval since 1995 when approval was at 73%.
>
> However, approval of hunting varies considerably depending on the stated reason for hunting. When the reasons are utilitarian in nature—for meat, to protect humans or property, for wildlife management—approval is very high, but hunting drops substantially when the reason is for the sport or for the challenge; meanwhile, less than a third of Americans approve of hunting for a trophy. Nonetheless, approval of these less popular hunting motivations has rebounded following rather sharp declines in 2016 (note that administration of the 2016 survey followed several high-profile news stories that depicted trophy hunting in a negative light).[14]

Ironically, most hunters in fact make a fuss about eating what they kill. In recent years, for example, there's been a surge in game cookbooks. The public's separation of hunting for food and sport hunting is an artifact of the way the questions were asked, but it is nevertheless revelatory. "Sport" suggests a trivial, self-indulgent activity—bluntly, killing "for the hell of it." The nonhunting public is largely unaware of the fact that the vast majority of hunters eat what they kill (the exceptions are "varmint hunters," who shoot crows or woodchucks, and hunters who hunt coyotes and other carnivores). Indeed, if you recall the elements of the fair chase enunciated over a century ago, one of them explicitly links utilizing the kill—including where possible the hide/fur as well as the meat.

Some writers have suggested that hunters drop the designation "sport hunters" or "sportsmen and women," arguing that "sport" carries connotations that nowadays trivialize the seriousness with which hunters take the hunt.[15] Hunters, they urge, should simply call themselves hunters and let it be at that. This doesn't mean disowning the origins of the term "sport hunter"; it just means acknowledging that in our day, "sport" has come to signify something that it didn't a hundred years ago. To be a "sportsman/woman" then meant that you hunted by a code of rules that were meant to honor wild game and emphasized the thrill of a fair chase over a focus on the kill. This reframing would be easier were it not for the fact that the public is treated to descriptions of trophy hunting and smiling hunters posed over their kill, which critics of hunting are only too adept at taking advantage of.

Despite the fact that a case can be made for well-regulated trophy hunting, it is also a fact that episodes like Cecil give hunters a black eye and can only diminish interest in hunting, especially the interest of young adults who do not come from hunting families and might reasonably be leery of being associated with activities that draw such public disapprobation. It is not a stretch to imagine the story of Cecil being told in one of the hunting magazines in the middle of the 1900s with a different twist—the story of a courageous bow hunter confronting a man-eating lion, mano a mano, wounding the animal, and then tracking the beast for days, never sure if the lion would attack. The magazines of the day routinely featured such stories, even though the subscribers, with few exceptions, would never be in a position to engage in such an adventure. But as we have seen, cultural norms have changed. What once would have been a thrilling adventure story is now a tale of vanity and ineptitude coupled with a bit of dubious legality.

The reputation of hunters has also suffered in recent decades because of another cultural shift, namely the increasing polarization of society, particularly in the United States, over guns and their regulation. We noted earlier that in recent decades as the polarization began in earnest, the number of guns in private hands has increased while the number of households in which there is at least one gun has dropped from a high in the late 1980s of nearly 50 percent to roughly a third today. There clearly is another shift in the culture with regard to guns, and there is no doubt that this diminishes parents' interest in encouraging their children to be interested in hunting. The polarization over guns is likely to have diminished young adult interest in hunting too.

Why has this polarization occurred?

One of the distinctive features of US history is the broad acceptance of guns in civilian hands, dating from the earliest colonies. Acceptance came with restrictions—no shooting across traveled ways, and no shooting near houses or outbuildings—commonsense precautions in the name of public safety. Acceptance did not mean everyone had a firearm. As historian Kevin Sweeney has painstakingly documented, gun ownership waxed and waned in colonial America, depending on local hostilities with natives, the reach of law enforcement, and the dependence on hunting and protecting domestic animals and crops.[16] Essentially, until the 1830s–1840s, muskets prevailed, but they required considerable maintenance to remain functional and were not particularly accurate. Frankly, they were no match for a skilled archer who could get off several arrows in the time it took to load a musket. Many of the firearms that Sweeney found in estate records were listed as non-functional. As Sweeney points out, these civilian firearms were distinct from those that were used by militias (and the British). The firearms suited to warfare were heavier and shot larger balls. The Second Amendment debate was about these military-grade firearms, not about the musket propped by the door to the chicken coop or carried into a marsh to shoot ducks. The framers were understandably concerned about firearms that could compete with the defenders of the state. Because of a shortage of military-grade muskets, General George Washington encouraged volunteers to bring their own muskets even as he deplored the condition and suitability of the muskets they brought with them.

Things changed dramatically in the first half of the nineteenth century. Advances in metallurgy, the innovation of rifled barrels (etched with grooves that caused the ball, and later the bullet, to spin as it traveled down the barrel, thereby significantly increasing the projectile's accuracy), and ultimately the perfection of the cartridge eliminated the need to charge the musket with powder (keep your powder dry), a wad, and the ball after each shot. Single-shot rifles soon became repeating ones, and the famous Colt revolver was capable of firing six shots before reloading. As important as these innovations were, they also represented an epochal change in manufacturing: machining parts to fine tolerances to create interchangeable parts marked the birth of mass production. Suddenly guns could easily be repaired, and if reasonably cared for, could last several lifetimes. (Jan's sons have several shotguns that were made a hundred years ago that are not just serviceable but coveted by hunters and collectors too.)

We have no reliable data on the extent of gun ownership after the Civil War, but we think it's safe to estimate that ownership increased over the pre–Civil War levels. Most guns were long ones (rifles and shotguns) used for hunting and some recreational shooting. Rifle competitions were a popular spectator sport both before and after the Civil War. (Don't forget the legendary Annie Oakley, who turned out crowds eager to see her outshoot male challengers.) With the proliferation of guns, a body of law emerged that distinctively reflected the United States. States, and ultimately the Supreme Court, argued over the legitimate use of firearms (not whether they could be privately owned). British common law basically said that a person had a duty to retreat from an assailant as long as retreat was possible. That position was steadily whittled away by US state courts, and by 1921, in an opinion written by Justice Oliver Wendall Holmes, the Supreme Court embraced the principle that, in Holmes's words in discussing his decision, "it is well established that a man is not born to run away."[17]

Enter the National Rifle Association (NRA). The NRA was begun in 1871 by a couple of army officers who served in the Civil War and were dismayed by the lack of *civilian* readiness in general as well as the lack of basic firearms adeptness among the Northern recruits. Their aim was to promote familiarity with guns along with the safe and effective use of them. Remember, this was a time when the United States did not have a standing army, and these generals were concerned about readiness, should the need arise—a concern that dates to the Washington and Jefferson administrations. For nearly a century, the NRA promoted hunting, gun safety, *and* laws that regulated the kinds of firearms and access to guns that today would be hotly resisted by the NRA. The NRA worked with summer camps, the Boy Scouts, and high schools and colleges across the country supporting shooting sports, hunting, and firearms safety. Then in the wake of the wrenching assassinations of John F. Kennedy, Martin Luther King Jr., and Robert Kennedy, not to mention the eruption of protests in the nation's inner cities, a flurry of legislative restrictions on the sale of firearms was passed. Within a couple of years, as antiwar protests racked the country and the civil rights movement helped ignite the women's movement, the nation started to divide as it hadn't since the Civil War. The new war was a "culture war," and decidedly uncivil.

In the early 1970s, the NRA was taken over by members who welcomed the culture war, and it began to lobby for relaxed regulations on access to guns. The organization continued to claim to represent the interests of hunters, but it prioritized a move more and more to the political Right. The heretofore nonpolitical organization began to support conservative candidates, many from the Sagebrush Rebellion who supported the NRA on unrestricted gun rights in exchange for tacit NRA support for conservative policies that promoted the resource exploitation of public lands, weakening of environmental protections, and hard-line opposition to any and all restrictions on access to guns. The NRA also became heavily dependent on financial support from the firearms industry, which was facing declining sales as the number of hunters started to decline.

While still boasting its support for hunting, the NRA began promoting self-defense. Fundraising appeals conjured images of rampant crime, race riots, and home invasions. After the 2016 election of Trump, the organization added the defense of the nation from the threat of socialism to the perils that people should arm themselves to prevent. It's worth noting that after Barack Obama's two presidential victories, gun sales spiked, but it's also important to remember that at the same time, fewer households had a gun.

Recently, the NRA has endured an investigation of its finances that has exposed lavish salaries for staff along with huge payments to lawyers and consultants, and is facing legal action that may result in its demise.[18] What's lost on the general public is that a minority of the nation's hunters are members of the NRA. (The NRA boasts a membership of five million; there are about eleven million hunters in the United States today.) More significantly, polls have revealed that the majority of hunters support gun laws that the NRA opposes.[19] It's fair to say that the NRA legitimately represented the interests of hunters for nearly a hundred years. It is clear that the NRA ceased being a reflection of most hunters' interests in recent decades too. Conservatives have wooed hunters by promising to protect their gun rights (against a supposed threat to seize all firearms) while eroding the policies and environmental protections that support robust populations of wildlife. But the connection of hunters with the NRA has saddled hunters with a reputation for supporting the NRA that is not warranted and, in some cases, unwanted. In the case of the latter, it's a burden that's hard to shake because many of the groups that support hunting and hunters remain dependent on the NRA as well as the firearms industry with which the NRA is closely linked and are loathe to criticize the NRA, lest they lose financial support. The increasing opposition to the NRA casts a shadow on all hunters, making it easy for critics of hunting to depict hunters as "right-wing gun nuts."

Even though the uptick in the number of women and young adult males who have been drawn to hunting bucks the trend, there is another threat that may slow that ray of optimism. Recent research by the Northwoods Collective has found that the new adults being attracted to hunting are overwhelmingly interested in big game hunting, mainly white-tailed deer.[20] A generation ago, two-thirds of US hunters were small game hunters (waterfowl, rabbits, and upland birds). The adult-onset hunters today have reversed this: two-thirds are involved in hunting big game. Project Upland, as the name suggests, is trying to reignite interest in upland hunting—pheasants, quail, grouse, doves, chukars, Hungarian partridge, and woodcocks. The boosters of small game hunting have an unwelcome ally, but an ally nonetheless: chronic wasting disease, a prion-based disease that is 100 percent fatal to deer (and related cervids).

As we noted in chapter 5, humans seem not to be at risk, but given the fact that mad cow disease, also a prion-based illness, takes many years to become symptomatic in humans (as much as ten to twenty years from exposure to death), many hunters have understandably become leery of consuming venison. This has thwarted attempts to enlist hunters in "herd reduction." Long steeped in the ethos of the fair chase, most hunters recoil at the prospect of turning a hunt into a slaughter, with the use of the meat by and large precluded. It is not inconceivable, though not imminent, that deer and elk hunting will become a dim memory, because of the near extinction of the species and/or the decline of interest in hunting a disease-ridden population.

Taken together, these demographic trends, cultural shifts, and pathogens do not portend a bright future for hunting, particularly the hunting that has been supported by the North American Model of Wildlife Conservation. It depends on a large number of hunters whose licenses and hunting-related purchases contribute to the state agencies that are crucial to hunting. Indeed, if habitat suitable for hunting continues to decline or access to it becomes commercialized, increased numbers of hunters would actually become a problem. Too many public areas open to hunting are already crowded, some to the point of being unsafe.

Continental hunting will likely persist since it does not depend on robust numbers of hunters. On the contrary, the major challenge continental hunters face is the critique of hunting launched by powerful animal rights organizations. The future of trophy hunting in Africa is similarly cloudy, with opposition mobilized on both sides of the Atlantic. Animal rights organizations have had less influence in the United States and Canada, where the defense of animals has less traction than the disparagement of hunters. As hunting becomes more expensive and burdensome, recruitment is likely to be modest at best, retention will also decline, and reactivation will be slight. This does not bode well for state agencies dependent on the sale of hunting licenses or the federal wildlife refuges supported by sales of the duck stamp. Pittman-Robertson Act revenues from the tax on guns, ammunition, and hunting paraphernalia remain high (though declining), but tellingly, about a decade ago over half of the revenues began coming from guns and ammunition sales used for purposes other than hunting, principally recreational shooting and personal defense.

In the late nineteenth century, US hunters faced a dramatic decline in game animals, and took the lead in mobilizing hunters and nonhunters to create the conservation movement that brought us parks, large tracts of publicly owned land, wildlife refuges, and game management strategies that sparked an unprecedented recovery of most game as well as many nongame wildlife species. In the early twenty-first century, hunters face many robust wildlife population, yet radically declining numbers of hunters. Might it be time to take a lesson from the past and create a new movement that links hunters with environmentalists? Might it be that hunters and the industries that depend on them won't be supported by more hunters? Might the future of hunting, in the United States and Europe, depend less on the numbers of hunters than on the amount of allies? By way of conclusion, let us explore this proposition.

As we have seen, there is a lot of mistrust of hunters by environmentalists, and the mistrust is reciprocal. The result has been the diminished influence of both groups. Landmark environmental laws like the Clean Air and Clean Water Acts have been weakened when they should have been strengthened. And as we've just noted, hunters have faced the loss of access to huntable areas, and several efforts to augment habitat for game species have been sharply rolled back (for example, the multistate accord to protect habitat for the greater prairie chicken) by conservatives determined to open as much public land as possible to mineral and fossil fuel exploration. Perhaps even more consequential for hunters, the proposed drastic weakening of the Clean Water Act, eliminating the protection of large chunks of the nation's wetlands, will almost certainly diminish crucial breeding habitat for waterfowl, and at the same time negatively affect pheasants, quail, and other game and nongame species that depend on wetlands along with the intermittent streams that provide habitat for breeding, raising young, and cover from harsh winters. These proposals are being challenged in the courts, and the election of President Joe Biden in 2020 will no doubt reverse some of these policies.

A rapprochement between hunters and environmentalists has begun. A number of the organizations representing hunters have joined environmental groups in challenging the weakening of environmental protections. Hunters and environmentalists, despite the suspicion and "bad blood," share a deep common interest in the protection of public lands, support for clean water, and protection of wildlife habitat. Hunters and environmentalists want to not only protect extant public lands but also extend protections to private lands through easements, conservation agreements, and land trusts. Ducks Unlimited has strongly opposed weakening the Clean Water Act that protects vital breeding habitat for migratory birds along with many other game and nongame species dependent on wetlands. Pheasants Forever has launched a campaign to restrict herbicides and insecticides that affect both pollinators and plants that pollinators as well as other beneficial insects (think monarch butterflies) depend on. This said, there are stumbling blocks.

One of the serious cleavages involves forestry policy. Many environmental organizations are against active forestry management practices. Many of the species that hunters pursue (and bird-watchers enjoy watching) depend on stands of early successional forests—the young saplings and underbrush that develop after natural or deliberate disturbance. The Ruffed Grouse Society has been a vigorous advocate of forestry management that produces early successional habitat. Some leading environmental groups, notably the Nature Conservancy, also support this, but other environmental groups are reflexively committed to defending old growth forests. In the face of serious loss of biodiversity, defending old growth against all other forest management goals is not only shortsighted; it ignores the fact that old growth is only one piece of the mosaic of our ecological heritage. One forest type does not fit all species of flora and fauna. And as we are painfully learning, homogeneously old forests, especially in the West, have become a tinderbox in part because of decades of fire suppression and opposition to timber harvests. To be fair, some opponents of logging are opposed to large-scale clear-cuts, which leave steep slopes exposed to erosion and invasive vegetation, and are critical of the US Forest Service, which has often favored the timber industry over broader environmental goals. That said, hunters and environmentalists could come to agree on forestry practices that are sustainable, and that support both loggers and biodiversity, and thus become a more effective counterweight to the timber industry.

The basic problem has been one of competing philosophies: the consumptive use of natural resources versus the preservation of them. Hunters, needless to say, tend to see natural resources in terms of consumption, as did the early conservationists. Environmentalists today are leery of consumption, though this has been changing of late. As just indicated, the Nature Conservancy, long an ardent advocate of preservation, has recently acknowledged that attempting to preserve or return landscapes to their pristine condition is no longer possible on a scale that would matter, and in many instances is not even desirable; intelligently managed, working landscapes are important too, and this includes hunting.[21] A focus on old growth and pristine landscapes is premised on the belief that nature was once stable—a belief, even without acknowledging thousands of years of human impact, that is simply wrong. Landscapes are dynamic. Humans have added to that dynamic, for better or worse. But there's no "going back." Like every other species, we depend on consuming what nature provides.

As we've seen in chapter 5, hunters still have a role to play in helping society deal with resurgent wildlife populations. The North American Model of Wildlife Conservation was a creature born of scarcity. It kept alive the democratic ideal of open access by encouraging hunters to embrace restraint. Restraint still matters, for ethical reasons, but for some species, notably white-tailed deer and geese, restraint has become problematic. There are too few hunters chasing too many deer and geese, and too many of the latter are now found in places that are not safely hunted. This situation presents an occasion for hunters and environmentalists to put their heads together to devise ways to deal with abundance. Living with wildlife sounds great, yet it's not a solution to goose-polluted parks and beaches, and it's not a solution to deer densities that exceed the capacity of the environment to absorb the impact of deer. Sport hunting alone may not offer a solution to these problems of abundance, but it's hard to imagine that hunters will have no part to play in managing wildlife populations that exceed the landscape's capacity to sustain them. Their role and that of the agencies that manage wildlife, though, are likely to change. Let's look first at the agencies and then turn to hunters who depend on those agencies.

As we have seen, critics of wildlife agencies have long claimed that the agencies devote disproportionate resources to service hunters' interests. With the current concern for the escalating loss of biodiversity, the critique is gathering new momentum. A recent article by Kevin Bixby, who identifies himself as an "occasional hunter who has spent [his] entire career in wildlife conservation," sharply criticizes the claim that since it's hunters' dollars that support the conservation work of the agencies, it's appropriate that hunters have a large share in determining policy. Bixby acknowledges that this claim was once true, and hunters' interests were at the core of what people understood as "conservation" in the United States.[22] But as we have had to say frequently, things have changed. The environmentalism awakened in the 1970s has grown and largely succeeded in expanding the meaning as well as reach of conservation. Bixby and others, some of whom are antihunters along with others who are not, urge that the funding for state and federal agencies be enlarged either from general revenues or taxes on other forms of outdoor recreation, including wildlife watchers, and that agencies broaden their work to vigorously promote biodiversity before it's too late.

Hunters would become one among equals contributing to the conservation of nature. This would no doubt expose some hunting practices to public scrutiny and disapproval. Bixby starts his essay with an account of a coyote killing contest in New Mexico, where he lives. Such contests are illegal in a few states, but coyote and prairie dog killing contests are held in a number of western states. Shooting animals over bait is also a controversial practice. As of this writing, twenty-two states permit baiting deer, and eighteen states permit baiting bears. Federal law prohibits the baiting of migratory birds.

The use of lead shot and bullets has also become controversial. Lead shot was banned by federal law for the taking of migratory waterfowl in 1991 after studies showed significant losses of ducks and geese to lead poisoning (via ingesting lead pellets inadvertently). Since then, calls for banning lead ammunition entirely have increased. California instituted a complete ban on lead ammunition for all hunting in 2019. Some states have banned lead on select public hunting areas, but lead is still widely used by both small and large game hunters. (Lead shot is cheaper and has ballistic properties that are preferred by many hunters, even though lead is toxic.) Some hunting organizations (Boone and Crockett most notably) have called on hunters to voluntarily shift to nontoxic ammunition. There is no reason to oppose a lead ban, other than a misplaced notion that a ban on lead ammunition is the proverbial slippery slope that leads to a ban on hunting. There is little evidence that the ban on lead has diminished waterfowl hunting. After initial resistance, waterfowl hunters, gun and ammunition manufacturers, and hunters adapted. It seems reasonable that hunters should embrace leaving lead behind, and by doing so, increase the likelihood of working together with environmental groups to promote policies that benefit both.

Another issue that has only recently started to surface involves the ammunition that bird hunters use. For decades, shotgun shells have been made of plastic, as have the wads that separate the shot from the powder inside the shell. The wads cushion the shot as it is propelled through the barrel, making the pattern of the shot more consistent by reducing the deformation of shot. Plastic hulls and wads also make reloading shotgun shells much easier, and the reloads are much cheaper than factory loads. The problem of course is that hunters have deposited tons of plastic wads and hulls cumulatively, and inevitably some of this plastic debris winds up adding to the pollution burden that we are all, hunters and nonhunters, inflicting on our environment and ourselves. Many hunters pick up their empty shells, either to reuse or clean up after themselves, but it is almost impossible to pick up even a tiny fraction of the millions of wads that are discharged over the course of a hunting season.

The death knell of lead was rung a generation ago when lead was banned for waterfowlers. The death knell for plastic is being rung today; local bans on single-use plastic bags are now common, worries about microparticles of plastic entering the food chain up to and including humans are mounting, and the evidence of fish and fowl being killed by ingesting plastic bits is now abundant. Hunters could easily gain support from environmental groups by joining them in insisting that alternatives to plastic shells and wads be sought. Industry will predictably resist, yet as with lead, it is clear that plastic shells and wads will eventually be declared illegal. Resistance will only make hunters seem reactionary, undermining their claim to be stewards of the environment.

This may be a more intractable problem than lead—for which there are now affordable and effective alternatives. It is hard to imagine that hunters would embrace a return to paper hulls and felt wads. Biodegradable plastics are now appearing on the market, but most simply degenerate into smaller and smaller particles, which raise their own problems for environmental and human health. Clearly, hunters should be calling on ammunition manufacturers to come up with alternatives to the conventional plastic hulls and wads, even though it will be a heavy lift.

We end on this note not to deepen the pessimism about the future of hunting (or give comfort to those who wish to see hunting banned) but instead to chart an ambitious and hopefully plausible course for a future in which hunting will be secure. Wildlife management and the agencies in charge are going to have to broaden their support beyond the ranks of hunters (and fishers) if they are to survive and be able to meet the daunting challenge of sustaining robust biodiversity. Hunters and the groups that represent them will have to accept these changes; it would behoove them to once again take a leadership role in this renewal of conservation. As we mentioned above, demonstrating a willingness to talk about lead and plastic could help build a new coalition that is sorely needed to ensure the future of the North American tradition of hunting: open access and science-based habitat and game management supported by license fees coupled with taxes on guns and hunting gear. Absent this, hunting in North America will come more and more to resemble hunting in Europe: highly regulated and limited to a small, largely affluent group. Hunting will persist, but a unique expression of democracy will be lost.

More broadly, killing wildlife will not end even if sport hunting were to be banned. We have seen that conflicts between humans and wildlife are ubiquitous, and in some places here and abroad, it's getting worse. There is a real risk of turning wildlife into pests to be dealt with

Demonstrating a willingness to talk about lead and plastic could help build a new coalition that is sorely needed to ensure the future of the North American tradition of hunting.

by exterminators; gone will be the role that the wild has played in our interactions with the natural world and our own sense of ourselves. In Leopold's terms, we will have completed the journey from being "plain citizens" in the biotic community to being "conquerors," turning over the engagement with the wild to hired professionals wielding guns, traps, and poisons.[23] We will have lost the humbling connection to the wild that has inspired the human imagination from the beginning. In an essay titled "A Theory of the Value of Hunting," environmental philosopher Paul Shepard suggested the importance of this:

> What does the hunt actually do for the hunter? It confirms his continuity with the dynamic life of animal populations, his role in the complicated cycle of elements . . . and in the patterns of the flow of energy. . . . Regardless of technological advance, man remains part of and dependent on nature. The necessity of signifying and recognizing this relationship remains. The hunter is our agent of awareness.[24]

Here and elsewhere in his writings, Shepard emphasized that hunting is not for everyone, at one point observing (with an unconscious nod to Artemis?) that hunting is like childbirth: a little of it can go a long way.

GLOSSARY

Bag limits
Caps on the number of deer, birds, and other game species that could be killed in a day and season. These restrictions were crucial in allowing game species to recover after the era of market hunting brought many species to the brink of extinction.

Chronic wasting disease
Like mad cow disease, chronic wasting disease is prion based. It attacks the central nervous system. Chronic wasting disease is limited to cervids (deer, moose, elk, and reindeer) and is communicated by close contact. The disease has no known cure and is 100 percent fatal. It is present in many states in the United States, several Canadian provinces, and reindeer and moose populations in northern Europe. So far there have been no known transmissions to humans, but many states are strictly regulating the transportation of cervids between states in an effort to contain the spread of the disease.

Culling
A management tool to deal with animals that have become too numerous in an area, causing habitat damage, disease, starvation, or property damage. Though sport hunters are sometimes enlisted in culling operations, this is not to be confused with sport hunting.

Fair chase
Codified in the late nineteenth century by socially elite hunters, the fair chase is a code of ethics that obliges the hunter to "level the playing field" by giving the prey ample opportunity to escape, making the hunt a contest between equals rather than an exercise in the dominance of the hunter over the hunted.

Game animals
Game animals are good to eat or challenging to pursue, or both. The distinction between them and nongame animals is arbitrary, deriving as much from local cultures as from any other set of criteria. Yet game animals are distinct from animals regarded as pests, or harmful to us or to our property (including our domestic animals and crops).

Hunting seasons
Seasons when game could legally be killed were established to protect animals when they were most vulnerable (during periods of breeding and rearing young).

Market hunting
Market hunting involves selling what is killed. It is generally associated with causing sharp reductions in the target species, and more recently, illegally killing animals (poaching).

Musket
Muskets are the original firearm. They shoot only one ball or a number of small pellets at one time. To ready a musket for firing, a measure of powder was poured into the barrel, followed by a patch of fabric or other material that would make a tight seal above the powder, and then the ball or pellets, all of which had to be tamped down so that when the powder was ignited by a spark when the trigger was pulled, the force released by the exploding powder would propel the ball or pellets toward the target.

Pot hunting
Pot hunting is a disparaging term referring to those who hunted merely for food, often contrasted to sport hunting.

Rifle
The rifle is a firearm developed in the early nineteenth century when the bullet was invented. The bullet put the primer (which starts the ignition of powder), powder, and projectile all in one casing. It didn't take long to invent rifles that could hold several bullets, making it unnecessary to reload after each shot.

Sport hunting
Distinct from both market and pot hunting, sport hunting emerged in the nineteenth century and emphasized the satisfaction of the chase rather than a focus on the kill. Sport hunting gave rise to the code of the fair chase.

NOTES

Chapter 1

1. Robert Ardrey, *The Hunting Hypothesis: A Personal Conclusion concerning the Evolutionary Nature of Man* (New York: Atheneum, 1976).

2. Richard B. Lee and Irven DeVore, eds., *Man the Hunter: The First Intensive Survey of a Single, Crucial Stage of Human Development—Man's Once Universal Hunting Way of Life* (Chicago: Aldine, 1968), 4.

3. Stephen Jay Gould, "Up against a Wall," *Natural History* 105, no. 7 (July 1996).

4. Jared Diamond, "Drowning Dogs and the Dawn of Art," *Natural History* 102, no. 3 (March 1993): 22–29.

5. This quote, and variations on it, has been widely cited but its authenticity has been questioned. See Paul Bahn, "A Lot of Bull? Picasso and Ice Age Cave Art," *Munibe Antropologia Arkeologia* 57, no. 3 (2005): 217–223, http://www.aranzadi.eus/fileadmin/docs/Munibe/200503217223AA.pdf.

6. Quoted in Mary Zeiss Stange, *Woman: The Hunter* (Boston: Beacon, 1997), 27.

7. Desmond Morris, *The Naked Ape: A Zoologist's Study of the Human Animal* (New York: Dell, 1969), 53.

8. Margaret Ehrenberg, *Women in Prehistory* (Norman: University of Oklahoma Press, 1989), quoted in Stange, *Woman*, 27.

9. Sherwood Washburn and C. S. Lancaster, "The Evolution of Hunting," in *Man the Hunter: The First Intensive Survey of a Single, Crucial Stage of Human Development—Man's Once Universal Hunting Way of Life*, ed. Richard B. Lee and Irven DeVore (Chicago: Aldine, 1968), 42.

10. Andree Collard and Joyce Contrucci, *Rape of the Wild: Man's Violence against Animals and the Earth* (Bloomington: Indiana University Press, 1988).

11. John Mackenzie, *The Empire of Nature: Hunting, Conservation, and British Imperialism* (Manchester: Manchester University Press, 1988), 2.

12. Lee and DeVore, *Man the Hunter*, 4.

13. James Gorman, "Ancient Remains in Peru Reveal Young, Female Big-Game Hunter," *New York Times*, November 4, 2020, https://www.nytimes.com/2020/11/04/science/ancient-female-hunter.html.

14. Michelle Rosaldo, "The Use and Abuse of Anthropology: Reflections on Feminism and Cross-cultural Understanding," *Signs: Journal of Women in Culture and Society* (1980): 389–417.

15. Donald Johanson and Edey Maitland, *Lucy: The Beginnings of Humankind* (New York: Simon and Schuster, 1981).

16. Walter Scheidel, *The Great Leveler: Violence and the History of Inequality from the Stone Age to the Twentieth-First Century* (Princeton, NJ: Princeton University Press, 2017).

17. Daniel Hillel, *Out of the Earth: Civilization and the Life of the Soil* (Berkeley: University of California Press, 1992).

18. A. W. Crosby, *The Columbian Exchange: Biological and Cultural Consequences of 1492* (Westport, CT: Praeger, 2003); Charles C. Mann, *1491: New Revelations of the Americas before Columbus* (New York: Knopf, 2005).

Chapter 2

1. Barbara Ehrenreich, *Blood Rites: Origins and History of the Passions of War* (New York: Metropolitan Books, 1977).

2. Richard Wrangham, *Catching Fire: How Cooking Made Us Human* (New York: Basic Books, 2009).

3. James Suzman, *Affluence without Abundance: The Disappearing World of the Bushmen* (New York: Bloomsbury, 2017); Bruce Pascoe, *Dark Emu: Aboriginal Australia and the Birth of Agriculture* (Melbourne: Scribe, 2018).

4. James C. Scott, *Against the Grain: A Deep History of the Earliest States* (New Haven, CT: Yale University Press, 2017).

5. Malcolm Margolin, *Life in a California Mission: The Journals of Jean François de la Perouse* (Berkeley, CA: Heyday, 1989), 24–25.

6. For a quick survey of these nongovernmental organizations, see forestpeoples.org, an umbrella organization that works with a wide range of Indigenous groups.

7. Marshall Sahlins, *Stone Age Economics* (New York: Routledge, 1972).

8. Hugh Brody, *Maps and Dreams* (New York: Pantheon, 1982).

9. Virginia Postrel, *The Fabric of Civilization: How Textiles Made the World* (New York: Basic Books, 2020).

10. Carolyn E. Boyd and Kim Cox, *The White Shaman Mural: An Enduring Creation Narrative in the Rock Art of the Lower Pacos* (Austin: University of Texas Press, 2016); Maxine Aubert, Rustan Lebe, Adhi Agus Oktaviana, Muhammad Tang, Basran Burhan, Hamrullah, Andi Jusdi, et al., "Earliest Hunting Scene in Prehistoric Art," *Nature* 576 (December 11, 2019): 442–445.

11. Richard Nelson, *The Island Within* (Washington, DC: Island Press, 1990).

12. Paul S. Martin, *Twilight of the Mammoths: Ice Age Extinctions and the Rewilding of America* (Berkeley: University of California Press, 2005).

13. Martin, *Twilight of the Mammoths*.

14. Shepard Krech III, *The Ecological Indian: Myth and History* (New York: W. W. Norton, 1999).

15. Charles C. Mann, *1491: New Revelations of the Americas before Columbus* (New York: Knopf, 2005); Scott, *Against the Grain*; Pascoe, *Dark Emu*.

16. Niles Eldridge, *Life in the Balance: Humanity and the Biodiversity Crisis* (Princeton, NJ: Princeton University Press, 1998).

17. Edwin N. Wilmsen, *Land Filled with Flies: A Political Economy of the Kalahari* (Chicago: University of Chicago Press, 1989).

18. Mann, *1491*, 189–191.

19. Pat Shipman, *The Animal Connection: A New Perspective on What Makes Us Human* (New York: W. W. Norton, 2011), 222.

20. Scott, *Against the Grain*, 107–108.

21. Walter Scheidel, *The Great Leveler: Violence and the History of Inequality from the Stone Age to the Twentieth-First Century* (Princeton, NJ: Princeton University Press, 2017).

22. Erich Hobusch, *Fair Game: A History of Hunting, Shooting and Animal Conservation* (New York: Arco Publishing, 1980).

23. Quoted in Hobusch, *Fair Game*, 35.

24. Judith M. Barringer, *The Hunt in Ancient Greece* (Baltimore: Johns Hopkins University Press, 2001).

25. Julie E. Hughes, *Animals Kingdoms: Hunting, the Environment, and Power in the Indian Princely States* (Cambridge, MA: Harvard University Press, 2013).

26. Quoted in Hobusch, *Fair Game*, 35.

27. Phillip Slater, *Footholds: Understanding the Shifting Family and Sexual Tensions in Our Culture* (New York: Dutton, 1977).

28. Suzman, *Affluence without Abundance*.

29. J. K. Anderson, *Hunting in the Ancient World* (Berkeley: University of California, 1985); Xenophon, *Anabasis* 5.3.7–10, quoted in Anderson, *Hunting in the Ancient World*, 31.

30. Hughes, *Animals Kingdoms*.

Chapter 3

1. James A. Tober, *Who Owns the Wildlife? The Political Economy of Conservation in Nineteenth-Century America* (Westport, CT: Greenwood, 1981).

2. Michael Zuckerman, "Pilgrims in the Wilderness: Community, Modernity, and the Maypole at Merry Mount," *New England Quarterly* 1 (1977): 255–275.

3. Daniel Justin Herman, *Hunting and the American Imagination* (Washington, DC: Smithsonian Institution Press, 2001), 14.

4. Herman, *Hunting*.

5. Andrea Smalley, *Wild by Nature: North American Animals Confront Colonization* (Baltimore: Johns Hopkins University Press, 2017).

6. Quoted in Smalley, *Wild by Nature*, 1.

7. Nicholas W. Proctor, *Bathed in Blood: Hunting and Mastery in the Old South* (Charlottesville: University Press of Virginia, 2002).

8. Smalley, *Wild by Nature*; Herman, *Hunting*; Tober, *Who Owns the Wildlife?*; William Cronon, *Changes in the Land: Indians, Colonists, and the Ecology of New England* (New York: Hill and Wang, 1983).

9. Herman, *Hunting*; Tober, *Who Owns the Wildlife?*

10. Quoted in Herman, *Hunting*, 15.

11. Cronon, *Changes in the Land*.

12. Otto Mayr and Robert C. Post, eds., *Yankee Enterprise: The Rise of the American System of Manufactures* (Washington, DC: Smithsonian Institution Press, 1981).

13. Phillip Dray, *The Fair Chase: The Epic Story of Hunting in America* (New York: Basic Books, 2018), 80–87.

14. Quoted in Dray, *Fair Chase*, 207.

15. Herman, *Hunting*; Dray, *Fair Chase*.

16. Garrett Hardin, "The Tragedy of the Commons," *Science* 162, no. 3859 (1968): 1243–1248.

17. Quoted in John F. Reiger, *American Sportsmen and the Origins of Conservation* (New York: Winchester Press, 1975), 28–29; emphasis in original.

18. George Perkins Marsh, *Man and Nature: Or, Physical Geography as Modified by Human Action*, ed. David Lowenthal (Cambridge, MA: Belknap Press of Harvard University, 1965).

19. William Cronon, foreword to *George Perkins Marsh: Prophet of Conservation*, by David Lowenthal (Seattle: University of Washington Press, 2000), xi.

20. Quoted in Dray, *Fair Chase*, 224–225.

21. Herman, *Hunting*, 229.

22. Quoted in Tara Kathleen Kelly, *The Hunter Elite: Manly Sport, Hunting Narrative, and American Conservation, 1880–1925* (Lawrence: University Press of Kansas, 2018), 148.

23. Reiger, *American Sportsmen*, 40–41.

24. Herman, *Hunting*, 278.

25. Kelly, *Hunter Elite*; Scott E. Giltner, *Hunting and Fishing in the New South: Black Labor and White Leisure after the Civil War* (Baltimore: Johns Hopkins University Press, 2008).

26. Karl Jacoby, *Crimes against Nature: Squatters, Poachers, Thieves and the Hidden History of American Conservation* (Berkeley: University of California Press, 2001).

27. Louis E. Warren, *The Hunter's Game: Poachers and Conservationists in Twentieth-Century America* (New Haven, CT: Yale University Press, 1997).

28. Giltner, *Hunting and Fishing*, 170–171.

29. "Fair Chase Statement," Boone and Crockett Club, accessed February 2, 2022, https://www.boone-crockett.org/fair-chase-statement.

30. John F. Organ and Valerius Geist, eds., *The North American Model of Wildlife Conservation* (Baltimore: Johns Hopkins University Press, 2019).

Chapter 4

1. Marc Boglioli, *Matter of Life and Death: Hunting in Contemporary Vermont* (Amherst: University of Massachusetts Press, 2009).

2. Doris Lin, "How Many People Are Killed or Injured in Hunting Accidents?," ThoughtCo.com, November 26, 2019. See also "Hunting Accident Statistics: Injury and Fatalities by U.S. States," Targettamers.com, February 14, 2020.

3. John R. Seeley, R. Alexander Sim, and Elizabeth W. Loosley, *Crestwood Heights: A Study of the Culture of Suburban Life* (New York: Basic Books, 1956).

4. Jan E. Dizard and Howard Gadlin, *The Minimal Family* (Amherst: University of Massachusetts Press, 1990), 64.

5. Dizard and Gadlin, *The Minimal Family*.

6. Betty Friedan, *The Feminine Mystique* (New York: W. W. Norton, 1963), 1

7. Dizard and Gadlin, *The Minimal Family*.

8. Adam Rome, *The Genius of Earth Day: How a 1970 Teach-in Unexpectedly Made the First Green Generation* (New York: Hill and Wang, 2013).

9. Aldo Leopold, *A Sand County Almanac* (New York: Oxford University Press, 1947).

10. Donald M. Waller and William Alverson, "The White-Tailed Deer: A Keystone Herbivore," *Wildlife Society Bulletin* 25 (1997): 217–226; Ron Baker, *The American Hunting Myth* (New York: Vantage Press, 1985).

11. Jon T. Coleman, *Vicious: Wolves and Men in America* (New Haven, CT: Yale University Press, 2004).

12. Christopher Ketcham, "The Rogue Agency," *Harper's Magazine*, March 2016, 39.

13. Leopold, *Sand County Almanac*, 138–139.

14. Peter Singer, *Animal Liberation: A New Ethics for Our Treatment of Animals* (New York: New York Review of Books, 1975); Tom Regan, "The Case for Animal Rights," in *Advances in Animal Welfare Science 1986/87*, ed. M. W. Fox and L. D. Mickley (Washington, DC: Humane Society of the United States, 1986), 179–189.

15. Franz De Waal, *Mama's Last Hug: Animal Emotions and What They Tell Us about Ourselves* (New York: W. W. Norton, 2018).

16. Adrian R. Morrison, *An Odyssey with Animals: A Veterinarian's Reflections on the Animal Rights and Welfare Debate* (New York: Oxford University Press, 2009); Susan Sperling, *Animal Liberators: Research and Morality* (Berkeley: University of California Press, 1988).

17. Joy Williams, "The Killing Game," *Esquire*, October 1990, 114, 121.

18. Marti Kheel, "License to Kill: An Ecofeminist Critique of Hunters' Discourse," in *Animals and Women: Feminist Theoretical Explorations*, ed. Carol J. Adams and Josephine Donovan (Durham, NC: Duke University Press, 1995), 39.

19. Matt Cartmill, *A View to Death in the Morning: Hunting and Nature through History* (Cambridge, MA: Harvard University Press, 1993), 239.

20. Jan E. Dizard, *Mortal Stakes: Hunters and Hunting in Contemporary America* (Amherst: University of Massachusetts Press, 2003).

21. Tom W. Smith, Michael Davern, Jeremy Freese, and Stephen L. Morgan, *General Social Surveys, 1972–2018: Cumulative Codebook* (Chicago: National Opinion Research Center, 2019).

22. US Fish and Wildlife Service, *2016 National Survey of Fishing, Hunting, and Wildlife-Associated Recreation*, October 2018, 113, 118, 28.

23. Stuart Marks, *Southern Hunting in Black and White: Nature, History, and Ritual in a Carolina Community* (Princeton, NJ: Princeton University Press, 1991).

24. Scott E. Giltner, *Hunting and Fishing in the New South: Black Labor and White Leisure after the Civil War* (Baltimore: Johns Hopkins University Press, 2008), 174.

25. These data are culled from the 2016 US Fish and Wildlife Service survey, the most recent data available.

26. Jan Ransom, "Amy Cooper Faces Charges after Calling Police on Black Bird-Watcher," *New York Times*, July 6, 2020, updated October 14, 2020, https://www.nytimes.com/2020/07/06/nyregion/amy-cooper-false-report-charge.html.

Chapter 5

1. Emma Marris, *Rambunctious Garden: Saving Nature in a Post-Wild World* (New York: Bloomsbury, 2011).

2. Oscar Wilde, *A Woman of No Importance* (London, 1893), act 1.

3. Marris, *Rambunctious Garden*, 57.

4. Patrick Barkhan, "Dutch Rewilding Experiment Sparks Backlash as Thousands of Animals Starve," *Guardian*, April 27, 2018.

5. Ann Mathews, *Where the Buffalo Roam* (New York: Grove, 1992); C. Josh Donlan, Joel Berger, Carl E. Bock, Jane H. Bock, David A. Burney, James A. Estes, Dave Foreman, et al., "Pleistocene Rewilding: An Optimistic Agenda for Twenty-First Century Conservation," *American Naturalist* 168 (2006): 660–681.

6. George Monbiot, *Feral: Rewilding the Land, the Sea, and Human Life* (Chicago: University of Chicago Press, 2014), 209–210.

7. Marris, *Rambunctious Garden*; Katharine Lackey, "Yellowstone's Wolves Are Back, but They Haven't Restored the Park's Ecosystem. Here's Why," *USA Today*, September 7, 2018.

8. Luke Harding, "170 Years On, Wild Bear Returns—to a Death Sentence," *Guardian*, May 22, 2006, https://www.theguardian.com/environment/2006/may/23/germany.conservationandendangeredspecies.

9. Glen Martin, *Game Changer: Animal Rights and the Fate of Africa's Wildlife* (Berkeley: University of California Press, 2012).

10. Martin, *Game Changer*; Mark Dowie, *Conservation Refugees: The Hundred Year Conflict between Global Conservation and Native Peoples* (Cambridge, MA: MIT Press, 2009).

11. Quoted in Christina Larson, "Lion Patrol: Learning to Share the Savannah with Big Animals," *ABC News*, October 8, 2019, https://abcnews.go.com/Technology/wireStory/lions-kill-cattle-people-kill-lions-cycle-end-66125642.

12. Daniel Botkin, *Discordant Harmonies* (New York: Oxford University Press, 1990).

13. Justin S. Bradshares, Peter Arcese, Moses K. Sam, Peter B. Coppolillo, A. R. E. Sinclair, and Andrew Balmford, "Bushmeat Hunting, Wildlife Declines, and Fish Supply in West Africa," *Science*, November 12, 2004, 1180.

14. Henry Wilkins and Danielle Paquette, "Burkina Faso's Wildlife Reserves Have Been a Battle Zone Overrun by Militants and Poachers," *Washington Post*, September 13, 2020.

15. Goodwell Nzou, "In Zimbabwe, We Don't Cry for Lions," *New York Times*, August 4, 2015, https://www.nytimes.com/2015/08/05/opinion/in-zimbabwe-we-dont-cry-for-lions.html.

16. Dowie, *Conservation Refugees*; Rosaleen Duffy, *Nature Crime: How We're Getting Conservation Wrong* (New Haven, CT: Yale University Press, 2010).

17. Associated Press, "More Than 1,000 People Killed in India as Human and Wildlife Habitats Collide," *Guardian*, August 1, 2017.

18. Caroline Alexander, "Tigerland: A Journey through the Mangrove Forest of Bengal," *New Yorker*, April 21, 2008.

19. Associated Press, "More Than 1,000 People Killed."

20. Botkin, *Discordant Harmonies*; Martin, *Game Changer*.

21. Ben Goldfarb, *Eager: The Surprising Life of Beavers and Why They Matter* (New York: Chelsea Green, 2018).

22. The following discussion is indebted to Jim Sterba, *Nature Wars: The Incredible Story of How Wildlife Comebacks Turned Backyards into Battlegrounds* (New York: Crown, 2012); Richard Nelson, *Heart and Blood: Living with Deer in North America* (New York: Knopf, 1997); Jan E. Dizard, *Going Wild: Hunting, Animals Rights, and the Contested Meaning of Nature* (Amherst: University of Massachusetts Press, 1999); Al Cambronne, *Deerland: America's Hunt for Ecological Balance and the Essence of Wildness* (Guilford, CT: Lyons Press, 2013); Jean-Louis Martin, Simon Chamaille-Jammes, and Donald M. Waller, "Deer, Wolves, and People: Costs, Benefits, and Challenges of Living Together" (unpublished manuscript, 2019).

23. Donald M. Waller and William Alverson, "The White-Tailed Deer: A Keystone Herbivore," *Wildlife Society Bulletin* 25 (1997): 217–226.

24. Paul D. Curtis and Kristi L. Sullivan, "White-Tailed Deer," Wildlife Damage Management Fact Sheet Series (Ithaca, NY: Cornell Cooperative Extension, 2001).

25. Sterba, *Nature Wars*, 127–134.

26. Sterba, *Nature Wars*, 127–134.

27. David Baron, *The Beast in the Garden* (New York: W. W. Norton, 2004).

Chapter 6

1. Ryan Sabalow, "Hunting Meshes Surprisingly Well with California's Progressive Values—and Now It's Fading Away," *Sacramento Bee*, February 20, 2020.

2. Michl Ebner, "The Economic Value of Hunting in the EU," Federation of Associations for Hunting and Conservation, 2016, http://www.face.eu/sites /default/files/documents/english/economia_della_caccia_27_9_2016_en.pdf.

3. Ebner, "Economic Value of Hunting in the EU."

4. Tovar Cerulli, *The Mindful Carnivore: A Vegetarian's Hunt for Sustenance* (New York: Pegasus Books, 2012).

5. Southwick Associates, "Covid-19 and Hunting License Sales" (report prepared for the Council to Advance Hunting and the Shooting Sports, April 2, 2021).

6. Jan E. Dizard, *Mortal Stakes: Hunters and Hunting in Contemporary America* (Amherst: University of Massachusetts Press, 2003).

7. David E. Petzel, "When Is It Time to Stop Pulling the Trigger?," *Field and Stream*, December 3, 2019.

8. Stephen R. Kellert, "American Attitudes toward and Knowledge of Animals: An Update," in *Advances in Animal Welfare Science*, ed. Michael W. Fox and Linda D. Mickley (Washington, DC: Humane Society of the United States, 1984–1985).

9. Corin Case-Carney, "Out-of-State Hunters Increase as In-State Decline," Montana Public Radio, November 15, 2019.

10. Michael S. Lewis, et al., "Selected Results from Surveys of Resident Deer, Elk, Antelope and Upland Game Bird Hunters regarding Hunting Access in Montana," Montana Fish, Wildlife and Parks, HD Unit Research Summary, No. 38, September 2014.

11. Henry Wilkins and Danielle Paquette, "Burkina Faso's Wildlife Reserves Have Been a Battle Zone Overrun by Militants and Poachers," *Washington Post*, September 13, 2020.

12. Wilderness Act of 1964, Pub. L. No. 88-577, 16 U.S.C. 1131-1136, § 2(c), https://www.fsa.usda.gov/Assets/USDA-FSA-Public/usdafiles/Environ-Cultural/wilderness_act.pdf.

13. Laura Helmuth, "Our Imperiled Oceans. Seeing Is Believing," *Smithsonian Magazine*, September 2008. See also Cara Giaimo, "Is There an Antidote to Shifting Baseline Syndrome?," *Anthropocene Weekly*, September 16, 2020.

14. Mark Damian Duda, Martin Jones, Tom Beppler, Steven J. Bissell, Amanda Center, Andrea Criscione, Patrick Doherty, et al., "Americans' Attitudes toward Hunting, Fishing, Sport Shooting, and Trapping," *Responsive Management*, 2019, https://www.fishwildlife.org/application/files/7715/5733/7920/NSSF_2019_Attitudes_Survey_Report.pdf.

15. Northwoods Collective, "A Look into the Mind of First-Generation Hunters," 2020.

16. Kevin M. Sweeney, "Firearms Ownership and Militias in Seventeenth- and Eighteenth-Century England and America," in *A Right to Bear Arms? The Contested Role of History in Contemporary Debates on the Second Amendment*, ed. Jennifer Tucker, Barton C. Hacker, and Margaret Vining (Washington, DC: Smithsonian Scholarly Press, 2019), 54–71.

17. Quoted in Richard Maxwell Brown, *No Duty to Retreat: Violence and Values in American History and Society* (Norman: University of Oklahoma Press, 1991), 36.

18. Brown, *No Duty to Retreat*.

19. Dizard, *Mortal Stakes*.

20. Northwoods Collective, "A Look into the Mind of First Generation Hunters."

21. Peter Kareiva and Michelle Marvier, *Conservation Science: Balancing the Needs of People and Nature* (Greenwood Village, CO: Roberts and Company, 2011).

22. Kevin Bixby, "Why Hunting Isn't Conservation, and Why It Matters," *Rewilding Earth*, 2020.

23. Aldo Leopold, *A Sand County Almanac with Essays on Conservation from Round River* (New York: Ballantine Books, 1970), 240.

24. Paul Shepard, "A Theory of the Value of Hunting," *Transactions of the Twenty-Fourth North American Wildlife Conference* (1959): 510–511.

BIBLIOGRAPHY

Alexander, Caroline. "Tigerland: A Journey through the Mangrove Forest of Bengal." *New Yorker*, April 14, 2008.

Anderson, J. K. *Hunting in the Ancient World*. Berkeley: University of California, 1985.

Ardrey, Robert. *The Hunting Hypothesis: A Personal Conclusion concerning the Evolutionary Nature of Man*. New York: Atheneum, 1976.

Associated Press. "More Than 1,000 People Killed in India as Human and Wildlife Habitats Collide." *Guardian*, August 1, 2017.

Aubert, Maxine, Rustan Lebe, Adhi Agus Oktaviana, Muhammad Tang, Basran Burhan, Hamrullah, Andi Jusdi, et al. "Earliest Hunting Scene in Prehistoric Art." *Nature* 576 (December 11, 2019): 442–445.

Bahn, Paul, "A Lot of Bull? Picasso and Ice Age Cave Art." *Munibe Antropologia— Arkeologia* 57, no. 3 (2005): 217–223. http://www.aranzadi.eus/fileadmin /docs/Munibe/200503217223AA.pdf.

Baker, Ron. *The American Hunting Myth*. New York: Vantage Press, 1985.

Barkhan, Patrick. "Dutch Rewilding Experiment Sparks Backlash as Thousands of Animals Starve." *Guardian*, April 27, 2018.

Baron, David. *The Beast in the Garden*. New York: W. W. Norton, 2004.

Barringer, Judith M. *The Hunt in Ancient Greece*. Baltimore: Johns Hopkins University Press, 2001.

Bixby, Kevin. "Why Hunting Isn't Conservation, and Why It Matters." *Rewilding Earth*, 2020.

Boglioli, Marc. *A Matter of Life and Death: Hunting in Contemporary Vermont*. Amherst: University of Massachusetts Press, 2009.

Botkin, Daniel. *Discordant Harmonies*. New York: Oxford University Press, 1990.

Boyd, Carolyn E., and Kim Cox. *The White Shaman Mural: An Enduring Creation Narrative in the Rock Art of the Lower Pecos*. Austin: University of Texas Press, 2016.

Bradshares, Justin S., Peter Arcese, Moses K. Sam, Peter B. Coppolillo, A. R. E. Sinclair, and Andrew Balmford, et al. "Bushmeat Hunting, Wildlife Declines, and Fish Supply in West Africa." *Science*, November 12, 2014, 1180–1183.

Brody, Hugh. *Maps and Dreams*. New York: Pantheon, 1982.

Brown, Richard Maxwell. *No Duty to Retreat: Violence and Values in American History and Society*. Norman: University of Oklahoma Press, 1991.

Cambronne, Al. *Deerland: America's Hunt for Ecological Balance and the Essence of Wildness*. Guilford, CT: Lyons Press, 2013.

Cartmill, Matt. *A View to Death in the Morning: Hunting and Nature through History*. Cambridge, MA: Harvard University Press, 1993.

Case-Carney, Corin. "Out-of-State Hunters Increase as In-State Decline." Montana Public Radio, November 15, 2019.

Cerulli, Tovar. *The Mindful Carnivore: A Vegetarian's Hunt for Sustenance*. New York: Pegasus Books, 2012.

Coleman, Jon T. *Vicious: Wolves and Men in America*. New Haven, CT: Yale University Press, 2004.

Collard, Andree, and Joyce Contrucci. *Rape of the Wild: Man's Violence against Animals and the Earth*. Bloomington: Indiana University Press, 1988.

Colson, Elizabeth. *Tradition and Contract*. New York: Transaction Publishers, 1974.

Cronon, William. *Changes in the Land: Indians, Colonists, and the Ecology of New England*. New York: Hill and Wang, 1983.

Crosby, A. W. *The Columbian Exchange: Biological and Cultural Consequences of 1492*. Westport, CT: Praeger, 2003.

Curtis, Paul D., and Kristi L. Sullivan. "White-Tailed Deer." Wildlife Damage Management Fact Sheet Series. Ithaca, NY: Cornell Cooperative Extension, 2001.

De Waal, Franz. *Mama's Last Hug: Animal Emotions and What They Tell Us about Ourselves*. New York: W. W. Norton, 2018.

Diamond, Jared. "Drowning Dogs and the Dawn of Art." *Natural History* 102, no. 3 (March 1993): 22–29.

Dizard, Jan E. *Going Wild: Hunting, Animals Rights, and the Contested Meaning of Nature*. Amherst: University of Massachusetts Press, 1999.

Dizard, Jan E. *Mortal Stakes: Hunters and Hunting in Contemporary America*. Amherst: University of Massachusetts Press, 2003.

Dizard, Jan E., and Howard Gadlin. *The Minimal Family*. Amherst: University of Massachusetts Press, 1990.

Donlan, C. Josh, Joel Berger, Carl E. Bock, Jane H. Bock, David A. Burney, James A. Estes, Dave Foreman, et al. "Pleistocene Rewilding: An Optimistic Agenda for Twenty-First Century Conservation." *American Naturalist* 168 (2006): 660–681.

Dowie, Mark. *Conservation Refugees: The Hundred Year Conflict between Global Conservation and Native Peoples*. Cambridge, MA: MIT Press, 2009.

Dray, Phillip. *The Fair Chase: The Epic Story of Hunting in America*. New York: Basic Books, 2018.

Duda, Mark Damian, Martin Jones, Tom Beppler, Steven J. Bissell, Amanda Center, Andrea Criscione, Patrick Doherty, et al. "Americans' Attitudes toward Hunting, Fishing, Sport Shooting, and Trapping." *Responsive Management*, 2019. https://www.fishwildlife.org/application/files/7715/5733/7920/NSSF_2019_Attitudes_Survey_Report.pdf.

Duffy, Rosaleen. *Nature Crime: How We're Getting Conservation Wrong*. New Haven, CT: Yale University Press, 2010.

Ebner, Michl. "The Economic Value of Hunting in the EU." Federation of Associations for Hunting and Conservation, 2016, http://www.face.eu/sites/default/files/documents/english/economia_della_caccia_27_9_2016_en.pdf.

Ehrenreich, Barbara. *Blood Rites: Origins and History of the Passions of War*. New York: Metropolitan Books, 1997.

Eldridge, Niles. *Life in the Balance: Humanity and the Biodiversity Crisis*. Princeton, NJ: Princeton University Press, 1998.

Friedan, Betty. *The Feminine Mystique*. New York: W. W. Norton, 1963.

Giaimo, Cara. "Is There an Antidote to Shifting Baseline Syndrome?" *Anthropocene Weekly*, September 16, 2020.

Giltner, Scott E. *Hunting and Fishing in the New South: Black Labor and White Leisure after the Civil War*. Baltimore: Johns Hopkins University Press, 2008.

Goldfarb, Ben. *Eager: The Surprising Life of Beavers and Why They Matter*. New York: Chelsea Green, 2018.

Gorman, James. "Ancient Remains in Peru Reveal Young, Female Big-Game Hunter." *New York Times*, November 4, 2020. https://www.nytimes.com/2020/11/04/science/ancient-female-hunter.html.

Gould, Stephen Jay. "Up against a Wall." *Natural History* 105, no. 7 (July 1996).

Hardin, Garrett. "The Tragedy of the Commons." *Science* 162, no. 3859 (1968): 1243–1248.

Harding, Luke. "170 Years On, Wild Bear Returns—to a Death Sentence." *Guardian*, May 22, 2006. https://www.theguardian.com/environment/2006/may/23/germany.conservationandendangeredspecies.

Helmuth, Laura. "Our Imperiled Oceans: Seeing Is Believing." *Smithsonian Magazine*, September 2008.

Herman, Daniel Justin. *Hunting and the American Imagination*. Washington, DC: Smithsonian Institution Press, 2001.

Hillel, Daniel. *Out of the Earth: Civilization and the Life of the Soil*. Berkeley: University of California Press, 1992.

Hobusch, Erich. *Fair Game: A History of Hunting, Shooting and Animal Conservation*. New York: Arco Publishing, 1980.

Hughes, Julie E. *Animals Kingdoms: Hunting, the Environment, and Power in the Indian Princely States*. Cambridge, MA: Harvard University Press, 2013.

"Hunting Accident Statistics: Injury and Fatalities by U.S. States." Targettamers.com, February 14, 2020.

Jacoby, Karl. *Crimes against Nature: Squatters, Poachers, Thieves and the Hidden History of American Conservation*. Berkeley: University of California Press, 2001.

Johanson, Donald, and Edey Maitland. *Lucy: The Beginnings of Humankind*. New York: Simon and Schuster, 1981.

Kareiva, Peter, and Michelle Marvier. *Conservation Science: Balancing the Needs of People and Nature*. Greenwood Village, CO: Roberts and Company, 2011.

Kellert, Stephen R. "American Attitudes toward and Knowledge of Animals: An Update." In *Advances in Animal Welfare Science*, edited by Michael W. Fox and Linda D. Mickley, 177–213. Washington, DC: Humane Society of the United States, 1984–1985.

Kelly, Tara Kathleen. *The Hunter Elite: Manly Sport, Hunting Narrative, and American Conservation, 1880–1925*. Lawrence: University Press of Kansas, 2018.

Ketcham, Christopher. "The Rogue Agency." *Harper's Magazine*, March 2016, 38–44.

Kheel, Marti. "License to Kill: An Ecofeminist Critique of Hunters' Discourse." In *Animals and Women: Feminist Theoretical Explorations*, edited by Carol J. Adams and Josephine Donovan, 85–125. Durham, NC: Duke University Press, 1995.

Kiernan, John S. "History of Credit Cards." WalletHub, April 5, 2021. https://wallethub.com/edu/cc/credit-card-history/25894.

Krech, Shepard, III. *The Ecological Indian: Myth and History*. New York: W. W. Norton, 1999.

Lackey, Katharine. "Yellowstone's Wolves Are Back, but They Haven't Restored the Park's Ecosystem. Here's Why." *USA Today*, September 7, 2018.

Larson, Christina. "Lion Patrol: Learning to Share the Savannah with Big Animals." *ABC News*, October 8, 2019. https://abcnews.go.com/Technology/wireStory/lions-kill-cattle-people-kill-lions-cycle-end-66125642.

Lee, Richard, and Irven DeVore, eds. *Man the Hunter: The First Intensive Survey of a Single, Crucial Stage of Human Development—Man's Once Universal Hunting Way of Life*. Chicago: Aldine, 1968.

Leopold, Aldo. *A Sand County Almanac*. New York: Oxford University Press, 1947.

Leopold, Aldo. *A Sand County Almanac with Essays on Conservation from Round River*. New York: Ballantine Books, 1970.

Lewis, Michael S., et al. "Selected Results from Surveys of Resident Deer, Elk, Antelope and Upland Game Bird Hunters regarding Hunting Access in Montana." Montana Fish, Wildlife and Parks, HD Unit Research Summary, No. 38, September 2014.

Lin, Doris. "How Many People Are Killed or Injured in Hunting Accidents?" ThoughtCo.com, November 26, 2019.

Lowenthal, David. *George Perkins Marsh: Prophet of Conservation*. Seattle: University of Washington Press, 2000.

Mackenzie, John. *The Empire of Nature: Hunting, Conservation, and British Imperialism*. Manchester: Manchester University Press, 1988.

Mandavilli, Apoorva. "Man-Eater Overload." *New Yorker*, May 26, 2014.

Mann, Charles C. *1491: New Revelations of the Americas before Columbus*. New York: Knopf, 2005.

Margolin, Malcolm. *Life in a California Mission: The Journals of Jean François de la Perouse*. Berkeley, CA: Heyday, 1989.

Marks, Stuart. *Southern Hunting in Black and White: Nature, History, and Ritual in a Carolina Community*. Princeton, NJ: Princeton University Press, 1991.

Marris, Emma. *Rambunctious Garden: Saving Nature in a Post-Wild World*. New York: Bloomsbury, 2011.

Marris, Emma. "Rethinking Predators: Legend of the Wolf." *Nature* 507 (March 13, 2014): 158–160.

Marsh, George Perkins. *Man and Nature: Or, Physical Geography as Modified by Human Action*. Edited by David Lowenthal. Cambridge, MA: Belknap Press of Harvard University, 1965.

Martin, Glen. *Game Changer: Animal Rights and the Fate of Africa's Wildlife*. Berkeley: University of California Press, 2012.

Martin, Jean-Louis, Simon Chamaille-Jammes, and Donald M. Waller. "Deer, Wolves, and People: Costs, Benefits, and Challenges of Living Together." Unpublished manuscript, 2019.

Martin, Paul S. *Twilight of the Mammoths: Ice Age Extinctions and the Rewilding of America*. Berkeley: University of California Press, 2005.

Mathews, Ann. *Where the Buffalo Roam*. New York: Grove, 1992.

Mayr, Otto, and Robert C. Post, eds. *Yankee Enterprise: The Rise of the American System of Manufactures*. Washington, DC: Smithsonian Institution Press, 1981.

Monbiot, George. *Feral: Rewilding the Land, the Sea, and Human Life*. Chicago: University of Chicago Press, 2014.

Morris, Desmond. *The Naked Ape: A Zoologist's Study of the Human Animal*. New York: Dell, 1969.

Morrison, Adrian R. *An Odyssey with Animals: A Veterinarian's Reflections on the Animal Rights and Welfare Debate*. New York: Oxford University Press, 2009.

Nelson, Richard. *Heart and Blood: Living with Deer in North America*. New York: Knopf, 1997.

Nelson, Richard. *The Island Within*. Washington, DC: Island Press, 1990.

Northwoods Collective. "A Look into the Mind of First-Generation Hunters." 2020.

Northwoods Collective. "The Word Sport in Hunting." 2019.

Nzou, Goodwell. "In Zimbabwe, We Don't Cry for Lions." *New York Times*, August 4, 2015. https://www.nytimes.com/2015/08/05/opinion/in-zimbabwe -we-dont-cry-for-lions.html.

Organ, John F., and Valerius Geist, eds. *The North American Model of Wildlife Conservation*. Baltimore: Johns Hopkins University Press, 2019.

Pascoe, Bruce. *Dark Emu: Aboriginal Australia and the Birth of Agriculture*. Melbourne: Scribe, 2018

Petzel, David E. "When Is It Time to Stop Pulling the Trigger?" *Field and Stream*, December 3, 2019.

Postrel, Virginia. *The Fabric of Civilization: How Textiles Made the World*. New York: Basic Books, 2020.

Proctor, Nicholas W. *Bathed in Blood: Hunting and Mastery in the Old South*. Charlottesville: University Press of Virginia, 2002.

Ransom, Jan. "Amy Cooper Faces Charges after Calling Police on Black Bird-Watcher." *New York Times*, July 6, 2020, updated October 14, 2020. https:// www.nytimes.com/2020/07/06/nyregion/amy-cooper-false-report-charge .html.

Regan, Tom. "The Case for Animal Rights." In *Advances in Animal Welfare Science 1986/87*, edited by M. W. Fox and L. D. Mickley, 179–189. Washington, DC: Humane Society of the United States, 1986.

Reiger, John F. *American Sportsmen and the Origins of Conservation*. New York: Winchester Press, 1975.

Rome, Adam. *The Genius of Earth Day: How a 1970 Teach-in Unexpectedly Made the First Green Generation*. New York: Hill and Wang, 2013.

Rosaldo, Michelle. "The Use and Abuse of Anthropology: Reflections on Feminism and Cross-cultural Understanding." *Signs: Journal of Women in Culture and Society* (1980): 379–417.

Sabalow, Ryan. "Hunting Meshes Surprisingly Well with California's Progressive Values—and Now It's Fading Away." *Sacramento Bee*, February 20, 2020.

Sahlins, Marshall. *Stone Age Economics*. New York: Routledge, 1972.

Scheidel, Walter. *The Great Leveler: Violence and the History of Inequality from the Stone Age to the Twentieth-First Century*. Princeton, NJ: Princeton University Press, 2017.

Scott, James C. *Against the Grain: A Deep History of the Earliest States*. New Haven, CT: Yale University Press, 2017.

Seeley, John R., R. Alexander Sim, and Elizabeth W. Loosley. *Crestwood Heights: A Study of the Culture of Suburban Life*. New York: Basic Books, 1956.

Shepard, Paul. "A Theory of the Value of Hunting." *Transactions of the Twenty-Fourth North American Wildlife Conference* (1959): 510–511.

Shipman, Pat. *The Animal Connection: A New Perspective on What Makes Us Human*. New York: W. W. Norton, 2011.

Singer, Peter. *Animal Liberation: A New Ethics for Our Treatment of Animals*. New York: New York Review of Books, 1975.

Slater, Phillip. *Footholds: Understanding the Shifting Family and Sexual Tensions in Our Culture*. New York: Dutton, 1977.

Smalley, Andrea. *Wild by Nature: North American Animals Confront Colonization*. Baltimore: Johns Hopkins University Press, 2017.

Smith, Tom W., Michael Davern, Jeremy Freese, and Stephen L. Morgan. *General Social Surveys, 1972–2018: Cumulative Codebook*. Chicago: National Opinion Research Center, 2019.

Southwick Associates. "Covid-19 and Hunting License Sales." Report prepared for the Council to Advance Hunting and the Shooting Sports, April 2, 2021.

Spies, Mike. "Secrecy, Self-Dealing, and Greed at the N.R.A." *New Yorker*, April 17, 2019.

Sperling, Susan. *Animal Liberators: Research and Morality*. Berkeley: University of California Press, 1988.

Stange, Mary Zeiss. *Woman the Hunter*. Boston: Beacon, 1997.

Sterba, Jim. *Nature Wars: The Incredible Story of How Wildlife Comebacks Turned Backyards into Battlegrounds*. New York: Crown, 2012.

Suzman, James. *Affluence without Abundance: The Disappearing World of the Bushmen*. New York: Bloomsbury, 2017.

Sweeney, Kevin M. "Firearms Ownership and Militias in Seventeenth and Eighteenth-Century England and America." In *A Right to Bear Arms? The Contested Role of History in Contemporary Debates on the Second Amendment*, edited by Jennifer Tucker, Barton C. Hacker, and Margaret Vining, 54–71. Washington, DC: Smithsonian Scholarly Press, 2019.

Tober, James. *Who Owns the Wildlife? The Political Economy of Conservation in Nineteenth-Century America*. Westport, CT: Greenwood, 1981.

US Fish and Wildlife Service. *2016 National Survey of Fishing, Hunting, and Wildlife-Associated Recreation*. October 2010.

Waller, Donald M., and William Alverson. "The White-Tailed Deer: A Keystone Herbivore." *Wildlife Society Bulletin* 25 (1997): 217–226.

Warren, Louis S. *The Hunter's Game: Poachers and Conservationists in Twentieth-Century America*. New Haven, CT: Yale University Press, 1997.

Washburn, Sherwood, and C. S. Lancaster. "The Evolution of Hunting." In *Man the Hunter: The First Intensive Survey of a Single, Crucial Stage of Human Development—Man's Once Universal Hunting Way of Life*, edited by Richard B. Lee and Irven DeVore. Chicago: Aldine, 1968.

Wilde, Oscar. *A Woman of No Importance*. London, 1893.

Wilkins, Henry, and Danielle Paquette. "Burkina Faso's Wildlife Reserves Have Been a Battle Zone Overrun by Militants and Poachers." *Washington Post*, September 13, 2020.

Williams, Joy. "The Killing Game." *Esquire*, October 1990, 113–128.

Wilmsen, Edwin N. *Land Filled with Flies: A Political Economy of the Kalahari*. Chicago: University of Chicago Press, 1989.

Wrangham, Richard. *Catching Fire: How Cooking Made Us Human*. New York: Basic Books, 2009.

Zuckerman, Michael. "Pilgrims in the Wilderness: Community, Modernity, and the Maypole at Merry Mount." *New England Quarterly* 1 (1977): 255–275.

FURTHER READING

Busse, Ryan. *Gunfight: My Battle Against the Industry That Radicalized America*. New York: Public Affairs Books, 2021.

Finney, Carolyn. *Black Faces, White Spaces: Reimagining the Relationship of African Americans to the Great Outdoors*. Chapel Hill: University of North Carolina Press, 2014.

McCaulou, Lily Raff. *Call of the Mild: Learning to Hunt My Own Food*. New York: Grand Central Publishing, 2012.

McDonald, Helen. *H Is for Hawk*. New York: Grove Press, 2014.

Nijhuis, Michelle. *Beloved Beasts: Fighting for Life in an Age of Extinction*. New York: W. W. Norton, 2021.

Posewitz, Jim. *Beyond Fair Chase: The Ethics and Traditions of Hunting*. Helena, MT: Falcon Press, 1994.

Schaller, George B. *The Serengeti Lion: A Study of Predator-Prey Relations*. Chicago: University of Chicago Press, 1976.

Stange, Mary Zeiss, ed. *Heart Shots: Women Write about Hunting*. Mechanicsburg, PA: Stackpole Books, 2003.

Syhed, Rebecca Wragg. *Kindred: Neanderthal Life, Love, Death, and Art*. New York: Bloomsbury, 2020.

INDEX

JAN E. DIZARD is Charles Hamilton Houston Professor of American Culture Emeritus at Amherst College. He is the author of books and articles on the changing family, race relations, and, of particular relevance to hunting, articles on environmental policy, hunting ethics, and wildlife.

MARY ZEISS STANGE is Professor Emerita of Women's Studies and Religion at Skidmore College. She is internationally recognized as the authority on women and hunting, and specializes in writing and speaking about women, guns, hunting, and ecofeminism.